SERVING & GIVING
GATEWAYS TO HIGHER CONSCIOUSNESS

OTHER BOOKS BY JOHN-ROGER, D.S.S.

Blessings of Light

Divine Essence

Dream Voyages

Forgiveness – The Key to the Kingdom

Fulfilling Your Spiritual Promise

God Is Your Partner

Inner Worlds of Meditation

Journey of a Soul

Living Love from the Spiritual Heart

Loving Each Day

Loving Each Day for Moms and Dads

Loving Each Day for Peacemakers

Manual on Using the Light

Passage Into Spirit

Psychic Protection

Relationships: Love, Marriage, and Spirit

Sex, Spirit, and You

Spiritual High *(with Dr. Michael McBay)*

Spiritual Warrior: The Art of Spiritual Living

The Consciousness of Soul

The Path to Mastership

The Power Within You

The Spiritual Family

The Spiritual Promise

Timeless Wisdoms, Vol. I

Timeless Wisdoms, Vol. II

Walking With The Lord

The Way Out Book

Wealth and Higher Consciousness

When Are You Coming Home? *(with Dr. Pauli Sanderson)*

OTHER BOOKS BY JOHN-ROGER, D.S.S. & PAUL KAYE, D.S.S

Momentum: Letting Love Lead

What's It Like Being You?

The Rest of Your Life

Mandeville Press
P.O. Box 513935
Los Angeles, CA 90051-1935
323-737-4055
jrbooks@**mandeville**press.org
www.**mandeville**press.org

Printed in the United States of America
ISBN# 978-1-893020-99-3

Photography: Dr. Jsu Garcia
Book Co-Design: Shelley Noble and Dr. Jsu Garcia

SERVING & GIVING
GATEWAYS TO HIGHER CONSCIOUSNESS

JOHN-ROGER, D.S.S.
WITH PAUL KAYE, D.S.S.

Mandeville Press

CONTENTS

Everybody can be great...
because anybody can serve.
You don't have to have a college degree to serve.
You don't have to make your subject
and verb agree to serve.
You only need a heart full of grace.
A soul generated by love.

MARTIN LUTHER KING JR.

When you help, you see life as weak.
When you fix, you see life as broken.
When you serve, you see life as whole.
Fixing and helping may be the work of the ego;
service, the work of the soul.

RACHEL NAOMI REMEN

If you were arrested for kindness,
would there be enough evidence
to convict you?

AUTHOR UNKNOWN

INTRODUCTION

In our culture we are more conditioned to get than to give. For every Mother Teresa who becomes famous for giving, there are hundreds of "heroes" who become famous for getting—getting rich, getting awards, getting high scores, getting elected. Even our English language proclaims that we "get married" rather than "give ourselves in marriage."

Giving, then, can feel uncomfortable—even unnatural and out of place in a society where consuming is more important than compassion, acquiring more important than bequeathing, and amassing more important than service. Yes, getting is also important to givers, but primarily so that they'll have more to give. Givers often hide their true natures of loving, caring, and sharing.

This book is about being okay with devoting a goodly portion of your life to giving, service, and kindness. This is not a book for everyone: only those who hear the call. If your desires run more towards *doing for* rather than *getting from*, you are not alone. Nor are you strange, weird, or unusual. You're just a giver and the "reward" you get is the opportunity to give more. And if that giving, loving, and serving can be done unconditionally, then you have the blessing of moving into higher consciousness.

If at any point while reading this book you think of someone who would enjoy receiving a phone call from you, a written note, or even a text message, or there is something you can do that would benefit another, please set this book aside and *call, go,* or *do.*

Accordingly, this book is comprised of brief chapters, making the book easy to put down. So put it down often so you can actually give and serve as often as you can, experience giving and serving firsthand.

The lessons in giving become available in the act of giving and serving, not in reading about it. The words in this book are here to inspire, motivate, and encourage so that you can give more in the ways that you know to give; and give in ways that you have never given before.

As you give, take notice of what you receive.

And, if there is anything you read here you disagree with—just disagree and drop it. Some things aren't for everybody. Take what works for you.

And if you never finish this book, may the reason be that you became too involved in giving, loving, and serving.

PART ONE:
The Life of Serving and Giving

" The purpose of human life is to serve, and to
show compassion and the will to help others. "

ALBERT SCHWEITZER

THE PURPOSE OF YOUR LIFE

I don't know what your destiny will be, but one thing I know: the only ones among you who will be really happy are those who will have sought and found how to serve.

ALBERT SCHWEITZER

Many people who come to me ask how they can learn to receive. But really what they are asking is how they can give in a way that is free from conditions, because when we give freely and unconditionally, we automatically create the place where we can receive.

The purpose of life is quite simply to live. The question then becomes, *how* are you going to live?

If, when contemplating your life purpose, you find words and concepts coming to mind such as service, sharing, compassion, loving, empathy, or kindness, you probably will not be truly satisfied until a goodly portion of your life is involved in giving and serving.

"When people are serving," wrote John Gardner, "life is no longer meaningless." When we give, at the very least, we are more likely to experience that our life has meaning; that we are living our life *on purpose*.

We sometimes *find* our lives in *losing* it in service to others.

START BY BEING A LITTLE KINDER

It's a bit embarrassing to have been concerned with the human problem all one's life and find at the end that one has no more to offer by way of advice than "Try to be a little kinder."

ALDOUS HUXLEY

What many great minds and hearts have concluded after a lifetime of discovery is that a simple act of kindness can be one of the most profound acts a human being can perform.

Speaking kind words is part of that. For what we say and the way in which we say it can be an important part of giving. Our choice of words and our tone of voice can calm, encourage, soothe, or inspire.

As Proverbs 16:23 points out, "A wise man's heart guides his mouth..."

Even criticism can be given in a positive way. I've seen a friend of mine, an actress famous for her physical allure, walk up to a strange man and say in his ear, "You're far too sexy to smoke," smile, and continue on her way. If I smoked, I would find this a much greater incentive to quit than someone lecturing me on how *bad* smoking is.

Sometimes uplifting words left on answering machines or notes of support written on a postcard take only a minute or two of our time but can provide hours or even days of encouragement to others.

Words are powerful. You are powerful. Giving is powerful. Imagine how powerfully helpful it can be when these three are combined.

DESTINED TO GIVE AND SERVE

The man who lives for himself is a failure. Even if he gains much wealth, position or power, he still is a failure. The man who lives for others has achieved true success. A rich man who consecrates his wealth and his position to the good of humanity is a success.

A poor man who gives of his service has achieved true success even though material prosperity or outward honors never come to him.

NORMAN VINCENT PEALE

While we are alive, our service never ends. We are destined to be of service. If you do nothing else, every time you exhale, you are being of service to the entire plant kingdom.

Animals take in oxygen and give off carbon dioxide. Plants take in carbon dioxide and give off oxygen. This mutual giving and receiving between the plant and animal kingdoms is one of the vital processes of life.

We give because not to give means death. Each time we exhale, we give carbon dioxide to plants: whichever plant gets it first, uses it. We may never receive anything directly from that plant; in fact, we don't even get to know which plant received it.

If, for some reason, however, you wanted to withhold your carbon dioxide from plants and hold your breath, soon it would hurt so much you'd give in and give. Even if you could withstand the pain, eventually you'd pass out. Then the plants would get your gift.

It's hopeless.

We are destined to give.

SOWING SEEDS OF KINDNESS

For every action there is an equal and opposite reaction. If you want to receive a great deal, you first have to give a great deal. If each individual will give of himself to whomever he can, wherever he can, in any way that he can, in the long run he will be compensated in the exact proportion that he gives.

R. A. HAYWARD

The person who sows seeds of kindness enjoys a perpetual harvest. One of the most difficult things to give away is kindness; it usually comes back to you.

The Hindus and most Eastern religions call it karma: what you do comes back to you.

The Christian version was stated by Paul: "For whatsoever a man soweth, that shall he also reap" [GALATIANS 6:7].

In the "hood," the same idea is simply stated, "What goes around, comes around."

This idea is such a universal and timeless one, that I would venture to put it into the category of "Truth."

If "what you sow you reap" is an answer, then the question is: "What kind of harvest would you like?"

THE COURAGE TO GIVE

That best portion of a good man's life,
His little, nameless, unremembered acts
Of kindness and of love.

WILLIAM WORDSWORTH

The word courage comes from the French *cœur*, meaning *heart*. We need great courage (heart) to give. Service is not for the faint of heart.

Giving is the easiest, most difficult thing you'll ever do.

In order to give, you must be willing to experience rejection and being misunderstood—not to mention the fear of rejection and the fear of being misunderstood, and the hurt of rejection and the hurt of being misunderstood, and the anger that covers the fear and the anger we turn against ourselves and the anger and sense of worthlessness that sometimes come when our gift is not found worthy.

In addition to pain, we must be willing to feel joy. Tolstoy (which rhymes with joy—but not very often) says that, "Joy can be real only if people look upon their life as a service, and have a definite object in life outside themselves and their personal happiness."

We came into this life and were given much: food, language, love, the world, the accumulated wisdom of humankind—especially the Internet, YouTube, and DVD players.

Generations yet unborn will appreciate what we have done, just as we appreciate what others who are long gone have done. There's no way to return the favor to posterity, but we can pass it on to the future.

DO YOUR DUTY

A hundred times every day I remind myself that my inner and outer life are based on the labors of other men, living and dead, and that I must exert myself in order to give in the same measure as I have received and am still receiving.

ALBERT EINSTEIN

Some consider doing for others a duty, the obligation we have to all life on this intricately interdependent world.

If you serve from a sense of duty, it's okay to enjoy yourself too. In fact, it's highly recommended.

LIGHT

Everything has a crack in it—that's how the light gets in.

LEONARD COHEN

Light is a concept that permeates all religions, most philosophies, and several sciences (quantum physics is based upon it). Stated simply, light is the energy that permeates all things. In the spiritual context, we refer to it as "the Light."

This Light responds to human thought and, more importantly, the intention of the heart.

One of the greatest gifts we can give is to "send the Light."

We can send Light, either to ourselves or to others, by saying or thinking, "I ask that the Light be sent to _____ (person's name) _____ for their highest good and the highest good of all concerned." That's all there is to it. That's sending the Light.

We add "for the highest good of all concerned" to keep our personal wants and desires (what we think is best) out of the situation. (As inconceivable as it may seem to our ego, we may not always know what's best for all people in all situations.) We send the Light "for the highest good of all concerned" so that in case our thoughts on how something should be happen to be slightly inaccurate, the highest good will nonetheless take place.

Sending Light for the highest good of all concerned allows us to relax. We can trust that whatever happens after sending the Light for the highest good of all concerned is for the highest good of all concerned. We need not feverishly manipulate the outcome to be whatever we think best.

MORE LIGHT

More light!

GOETHE'S LAST WORDS

A simple way to be of service is to send the Light for the highest good. You can do that now—to yourself, your family, your co-workers, your pets, your country, the planet.

Sending the Light—to yourself, to another, or to a situation—can be done anywhere, at any time. It takes only a second (literally). The next time you're put on hold, don't just hold your temper; send the Light. The next time you're detained at a traffic light, send the Light. The next time you're standing in line, consider it a "send-the-Light line."

The strange thing about it is, you are to be there for some reason, if only to have the Light come through that area. Just as the lights of your car shine down the road. That's it. It's not for you to know the value of what happened. It's just yours to drive down the road. Those are opportunities for silent service and we all can do a lot of that. Just a great deal of the time.

Before setting out to physically be of service, we suggest that you ask the Light to fill, surround, protect, bless, and heal you for your highest good, the highest good of all you come into contact with, and the highest good of all concerned. This "armor of Light" acts both as a shield and as a vehicle through which some of our more profound gifts can be given.

Light lightens the load and Lights the path.

THE GIFT OF GIVING

Getters generally don't get happiness; givers get it.

You simply give to others a bit of yourself—
a thoughtful act, a helpful idea, a word of appreciation,
a lift over a rough spot, a sense of understanding,
a timely suggestion.

CHARLES H. BURR

At first, we may give because it is the "right" thing to do. Later, we give because giving feels good. Eventually, we give because, well, that's just what we do. At that time, the giver and the gift become one.

What is the most beautiful gift you can give? The gift of yourself.

We can get so caught up in trying to find the perfect gift or the right words to say to someone, yet the simplest and most precious gift you have to give resides within you.

That can be difficult to accept. We tend to look outside ourselves and compare. Everyone else seems to have more talent, money, happiness—more of everything we think we want. Yet, the reality is that everything you've ever wanted or dreamed of having is already present within you.

When we think our fulfillment is "out there" we start the search for what is "missing" from us. By taking the inner journey, gifts will be revealed and give you more than you thought was possible.

You may be blind to your own gifts but within yourself, you can become acquainted and familiar with your true nature and gain the skills and confidence to use your inherent gifts.

Every day, in every way, you are enough. Even though you may have habits you'd like to change, physical features you don't like, or a mind that wanders when you want it to stay focused, who you really are shines forward more brightly than any judgments you hold against yourself.

Have the courage to be you. Create enough love to accept every part of yourself. And as you give these gifts to yourself, the more you will receive.

You are a portable gift ready to participate at any given moment. It may be by giving a smile or by simply being patient. While one person has the gift of laughter, another person blesses us with the silence and peace they exude. Each one of us is important!

Appreciate the gifts you have been given and the gifts you have to share. Be grateful for who you are.

It is indeed a blessing that we all have an abundance of gifts to share with each other.

THE BEST WAY TO "LIKE" SOMEONE

*It is one of the beautiful compensations of this life
that no one can sincerely try to help another without
helping himself.*

CHARLES DUDLEY WARNER

Sometimes we have trouble liking others—loving is no problem; it's liking that's tough.

"I love humanity," someone once observed, "it's people I can't stand."

For givers, the best way to like someone is to do something for them. We know this goes against conventional wisdom, but givers, as you may have noticed, find wisdom in unconventional ways.

THE TAKERS MAY EAT BETTER,
BUT THE GIVERS SLEEP BETTER

They who give have all things;
they who withhold have nothing.

What we give returns to us. What we give, then, determines the currents and the currency of our lives.

What do you want most? Loving? Compassion? Caring? Tenderness? Laughter? Joy? Money? Whatever it is (or they are), give it away.

When it returns, you can choose to "spend" it, (use it, enjoy it, feel it, and so on), or you can give it away again. Certainly, you can enjoy it while it passes through your hands—or heart. Given away, it returns again, and usually faster than the first time. Give it away again, and it returns again. Give, return. Give, return.

Soon it's hard to tell whether all that loving, compassion, caring, tenderness, laughing, joy, and money is coming or going.

Eventually, it's not a matter of giving and then receiving love, but it all merges into a steady flow of loving. There is no beginning or ending.

THE NEED TO GIVE

There are two kinds of gratitude:
The sudden kind we feel for what we take;
the larger kind we feel for what we give.

E. A. ROBINSON

One of the most eloquent expressions of our need to give was published in Harry Emerson Fosdick's 1920 book, *The Meaning of Service*. He uses an analogy from the Holy Land—two seas that offer a parallel to human life:

The Sea of Galilee and the Dead Sea are made of the same water.

It flows down, clear and cool, from the heights of Hermon and the roots of the cedars of Lebanon.

The Sea of Galilee makes beauty of it, for the Sea of Galilee has an outlet.

It gets to give.

It gathers in its riches that it may pour them out again to fertilize the Jordan plain.

But the Dead Sea with the same water makes horror. For the Dead Sea has no outlet.

It gets to keep.

THE PRIVILEGE OF SERVING

When you cease to make a contribution, you begin to die.

ELEANOR ROOSEVELT

It is a *privilege* to serve. Each time we give, we are affirming, "Thank you; I have more than I need."

Eleanor Roosevelt saw death not just as physical departure but more of the gradual dimming of our inner Light, our connectedness to life, our relations with ourselves and with everyone and everything around us.

To paraphrase Mrs. Roosevelt, you begin to die the first time you are asked to give, are able to give, know it's for the highest good, and yet you don't.

It is a slow death. Some people have it so well justified that their selfishness has become a code of honor. That is too bad. I wonder what we can do to serve them.

CURMUDGEONLY GIVING

Behold, I do not give lectures or a little charity,
When I give I give myself.

WALT WHITMAN

Giving is not just something goody-goody people do: some of the greatest curmudgeons of all time have acknowledged the fact that we do good because *it's good for us.*

It wouldn't be much fun to own everything in the world, while everyone else had nothing. With most people willing to give a little, the world turns a lot easier. A little giving makes a more enjoyable world, so we give—like it or not—because we do like living in a better world.

For example, someone may stop us and ask directions, and we may not feel like giving directions. If nobody ever gave directions, however, it would be hard to get around. So we take the time and give the directions. We prefer living in a world where it's easier to get around.

If nobody gave, this would be an ugly world. So, not liking ugly, we give.

Besides, as Sir Philip Gibbs wittily observed, "It's better to give than to lend, and it costs about the same."

WHEN DO I GET MINE?

Lose yourself in generous service and every day
can be a most unusual day, a triumphant day,
an abundantly rewarding day!

WILLIAM ARTHUR WARD

You may say, "But when do I get mine?" With that attitude, however, you're never likely to get yours. How about helping somebody else get theirs?

If you help them get theirs, *then* do you get yours?

It doesn't work that way.

The highest form of consciousness is service. And the highest form of service is selfless service. Find someone to serve. Just do a random act of kindness without any expectation of anything coming back to you for any reason.

Do you know what a random act of kindness might look like? Leaving someone alone.

It might also look like asking them if there is anything you can do to assist them in some way. That way, you leave an opening.

Whatever it takes is whatever it takes. Personally I don't know what it takes. I just know you keep going until the other person says, "That's fine, thank you."

I take them at their word and then move on to serve others.

HOW MUCH DO WE GIVE?

We are here on earth to do good to others.
What the others are here for, I don't know.

W. H. AUDEN

How much we give depends on how much we've been given: from whom much has been given, much is expected.

Those who are given much, or given the gift of making much, can, if they choose, become big consumers: more houses, bigger houses; more cars, more expensive cars; boats, limos, private jets.

Those who have lived the life of material excess know it is not a life of luxury: it is a life of *maintenance*. A life of obtaining soon becomes a life of *maintaining*. Keeping up with the Joneses also means keeping up all that *stuff.*

"Luxury comes as a guest," as the Hindu proverb states, "and soon becomes the master."

Luckily, some who have been given much have also been given the wisdom to see that the excess (be it an excess of money, ability, ideas, love, humor, or anything else we possess in abundance) was given to us so that we might have the joy of giving it away.

Receiving is joyful, but giving is blissful. Whatever we've been given in abundance, inherent in that gift is the bliss of giving away our overflow.

WHAT IS SERVICE?

Consciously or unconsciously, every one of us does render some service or another. If we cultivate the habit of doing this service deliberately, our desire for service will steadily grow stronger, and it will make not only for our own happiness but that of the world at large.

MAHATMA GANDHI

Let me be clear you don't *have* to serve for long hours. Maybe your service is in increments.

Maybe you do it fifteen minutes one day and another day you do it for a half hour. Maybe you miss for three or four days and then you have five minutes and you are nice to a little kid that really needs to have somebody be nice to him.

You can even be of service whether or not you really care that much—but don't let the person know that you don't. Let them feel the caring. Then, whether you were of service or not in your own mind, you were of service in that one's mind. That's what is really important.

You see there is no one definitive answer of what service is. It's really relative to the situation. It is so circumstantial. The one thing we know about it is that *being* of service is really the *doing* of service.

THE KEY FOR THIS DISPENSATION

You give but little when you give of your possessions.
It is when you give of yourself that you truly give.

KAHLIL GIBRAN

As you serve unconditionally, you become your heart, your soul, and you become the heart of others; in that you will know what people need and how to meet them with the Spirit.

This takes place when you are attuned to your spiritual heart, and it is a moment-to-moment process that unfolds as you trust the Spirit and move with it.

You may reach out to another person's heart with a kind word or loving touch, and then wonder whether you did the right thing. You do the right thing when you are attuned to your Spirit.

The willingness to do gives you the ability to do. Do you understand that? It's the key for this dispensation of the next 2,000 years. Here it is again:

The willingness to do gives the ability to do.

Whenever you are just willing to follow your heart, even though you don't know the details of what you are doing, it works out. It works because the willingness to do gives you the ability to do and you surprise yourself.

I don't run perfection; I just do.

Sometimes the grandiosity of our visions doesn't match our ability to do. So we fall short and then tell people the great vision and how we failed, usually managing to blame others in the process. Just forget about the failures and forget about the vision and do what's in front you. Your willingness will give you the ability.

SLAVING VERSUS SERVING

It follows that the richer, the wiser, the more powerful
a man is, the greater is the obligation upon him to
employ his gifts in lessening the sum of human misery.

JOHN RANDOLPH

You know I don't think anybody wants to be your slave this year.

I'm sure you don't want to be anybody else's slave either. But I'm equally sure that all of us are willing to serve the one we love at our greatest capacity… not slave—serve.

That means as we serve, they have to be big enough to receive, and then when they serve us, we've got to be big enough to receive.

If you're not big enough to receive what is being served to you, then you're not learning how to grow.

If you are looking at life as fulfilling your sensual needs and you want to walk through life with a sense of entitlement with everyone serving you, that's Utopia.

Utopia does not exist here. It cannot exist here. Utopia is a crippling process—as soon as you want it, it's delivered. That's called "hell" because you get everything you want. After awhile, you've got so much of everything, you don't know what it is you want, and now it's called "boring."

To work for things in a relationship brings a sense of esteem when you've done the right thing, with the right motive, and an attitude of heartfelt service.

Life suddenly becomes magical and you experience fulfillment.

24

AN ADDITIONAL COMPENSATION

When you find yourself overpowered, as it were,
by melancholy, the best way is to go out and do
something kind to somebody or other.

JOHN KEBLE

Walking through the many dark valleys in this life—pain, sorrow, loss, hurt, anger, worry, frustration, illness, and the rest—all people gain value by

(a) surviving them,
(b) overcoming them, and one hopes,
(c) learning something from them.

Givers, however, have an additional compensation: they can use the experience and what they've learned to be of greater service to others.

Givers become more compassionate. They can say to someone, "I've been there," and the other person will know they speak the truth.

Givers are more understanding. Where the less experienced might say, "Oh, just snap out of it," givers might know that "snapping out of it" is not an option for this person at this time.

Givers are more able to be with a person, to let the person know he or she is not alone, to help the person believe that healing lies ahead. They might even be able to offer suggestions that can speed the healing along.

HOW MUCH IS ENOUGH?

You have not done enough,
you have never done enough,
so long as it is still possible that you
have something to contribute.

DAG HAMMARSKJOLD

If you see service as a painful duty, then Dag Hammarskjold's quote above must read like a sentence of doom.

If, however, you believe that service is bliss, then Mr. Hammarskjold's comment is a joyful thought: we will have the opportunity to give right up until the end of our lives. (And who knows whether the end is not just another beginning?)

Even at the end of our lives, we can serve others by *allowing them to serve us.*

As we come to the end of part one, have you got that urge to serve yet?

PART TWO
Serving and Giving to the Self

❝ For it is in giving that we receive. ❞

ST. FRANCIS OF ASSISI

TO YOUR OWN SELF BE TRUE

The best way to find yourself
is to lose yourself in the service of others.

MOHANDAS K. GANDHI

The answer to our world problems at this time on this planet, as simple as it may sound, is forgiveness. For give-ness.

Serving yourself is being forgiving to yourself. If I am truly forgiving towards myself, I will also be forgiving to others. I am also forgiving anything they did; otherwise, I'd be saying that they are not worth enough for me to give to. My forgiving says that they are fine as they are.

God gives that unconditional acceptance to us. He says, "You're fine as you are," because He keeps us going.

People ask me, "How do you live?" My answer is, "In a state of forgiveness." When they ask, "How do you make your living?" I say, "Forgiving."

As long as your priority is to think about yourself and what your wants and needs and desires are, over finding time to serve other people, you don't find who you are, truly. It's in serving that we find ourselves.

To your own Self be true. Forgive and serve.

BE GOOD TO YOURSELF

The most difficult part is to give
Then why not add a smile?

JEAN DE LA BRUYERE

Take good care of yourself.

Be good to yourself.

The God inside of you can only be touched through goodness.

Just be free. Then the next step appears.

All the true religions back through time had, in their essence, the basic principles of service, love, and devotion. And along with that would be caring.

That includes caring for yourself.

Serving yourself is letting yourself be.

That is high service.

Goodness, if people just let themselves be.

That state of being is absolutely majestic.

TAKING CARE OF YOURSELF

The deed is all, not the glory.

GOETHE

A common perception, and perhaps it is something we grew up with, is the mentality of, "I gave you something—now you're going to have to give something back to me. You owe me." This is a trading situation, rather than giving. And it probably makes up most of the way people approach our world today.

The more fulfilling approach is to not only give but also to observe how people receive the giving, and what they do with it. I have seen a person look ten years younger, instantly, by getting free of something that was disturbing them.

All that took place was a simple service to them. But it was done in a loving, giving, unconditional way. I look at service and the consciousness of serving as being the highest one on the planet that we can see. Someone truly serving another human being with loving is a joy to behold.

Of course, throughout history there were those people who got so much into service that they became martyrs and forgot about taking care of themselves. So we have three groundrules to live your life by:

1) *Take care of yourself, so you can help take care of others.*

2) *Don't hurt yourself, and don't hurt others.*

3) *Use everything for your upliftment, learning, and growth.*

Within these three groundrules is a regenerative approach that allows you to serve and give to others in a balanced way.

TAKING TIME FOR YOURSELF

Kindness is never wasted.
If it has no effect on the recipient,
at least it benefits the bestower.

Kindness can become its own motive.
We are made kind by being kind.

ERIC HOFFER

Serving yourself is taking time for your Self. It may be having some moments of silence meditating, doing spiritual exercises (see glossary). Or it could be forgiving yourself for judgments you have placed against yourself or others.

It's taking time for your Self, so that your cup can be refilled. Then you can serve again from the fullness and give of your overflow.

The emphasis is on Self, not self. Many people see taking care of themselves as indulging themselves. That can work, but it often fails because it caters to the mind and emotions that always want more.

Giving to your Self is renewing, regenerating, and rejuvenating. You fill your Self so you can give of the overflow.

You take care of your Self so you can then help take care of others.

SERVING YOUR SELF

When you truly give up trying to be whole
through others, you end up receiving what
you always wanted from others.

SHAKTI GAWAIN

One of the most wonderful forms of service is service to yourself.

How do you serve your self? If you have been negative, you own it.

How do you clear it? By immediately involving yourself with serving someone else.

This is the best way to overcome negativity because when you serve you put your worries and your pettiness aside. Thus, you become a positive reference point for the person you serve, and you become a positive reference point for yourself.

You can serve in a simple way through a loving gesture. Make someone a cup of tea, and *poof,* there goes the negativity.

If it's so easy why do you have negativity?

Because you sit down and bemoan that you're a victim. You don't have to do anything when you declare yourself a victim.

WHY IS IT SUCH FUN TO GIVE?

Giving is more joyous than receiving,
not because it is a deprivation, but because in
the act of giving lies the expression of my aliveness.

ERICH FROMM

If you give with no ulterior motives, the look on the person's face who receives is such a wonderful thing to see. It's like Christmas—every day.

Giving and service are not necessarily the same, but they are Siamese twins. You can serve begrudgingly, and you can give and expect a return. But what I'm talking about is where you give and you don't expect anything in return. You just give because there's loving and giving inside of you, and why wouldn't you do that?

You look at everybody as your brother or your sister. Why wouldn't you give what you can?

And when you can't, you don't. You don't have to explain it. But you might want to say, "I don't have it to give right now."

That's taking care of yourself, which is serving yourself.

THE GIFT OF RECEIVING

There never was a person who did anything worth doing who did not receive more than he gave.

HENRY WARD BEECHER

There is a difference between giving a present to someone and giving the gift of your giving, which is the gift of your loving heart.

There is a difference between getting a present from someone and giving that person the gift of receiving their loving heart.

If you weigh the value of the gift in your mind and equate it with the giver's love for you, you sell yourself short and you sell them short.

I look at a gift as an extension of a person's heart, and I don't value the gift as much as I value the heart of the giver. I open my heart and receive the physical gift, which then allows them to also send their heart into my heart, spiritually.

I will sacrifice *anything* to get to that loving heart, to awaken you to your loving heart, and to have you open your heart to the divine melodies that sing inside of you. The divine melodies of God sing of the loving heart. The loving heart encompasses all the rest; it encompasses peace, joy, Light, justice, truth... and the grace of the Lord. The loving heart loves unconditionally. It holds back nothing.

Give the gift of giving yourself to others and the gift of receiving the self of others. That is loving made active and alive. God lives inside of you, as you; and you can receive that personal experience of God in every moment.

LEARNING TO RECEIVE

*If my hands are fully occupied in holding on
to something, I can neither give nor receive.*

DOROTHEE SOLLE

You must be open to receive. If I have something to give you but your hands are tightly closed and clenched behind your back, I have no vessel in which to place my gift. But if your hands are open and you reach out to receive, I can place the gift in them.

The same is true for those things that are of Spirit. If you are uptight and closed down inside of yourself, how can you be open to receive the bounty that is available to you?

If it's truly difficult for you to receive, you might begin by receiving in small ways. Let someone buy you lunch, open the door, or run an errand for you. Most people will be very willing to give to you. It's you who decides how much you want to receive on all levels.

Out of thankfulness, you build the ability to receive. And then you give, and that giving allows the receiving also.

It is a process, one that you can practice daily.

KEEP THE HOME FIRES BURNING

To keep a lamp burning we have to keep putting oil in it.

MOTHER TERESA

Naturally, before we can be of service to others, we must be of service to ourselves. If we don't, eventually someone will have to be of service to us.

The extreme example would be someone who is so busy giving and giving and giving that they take no time for rest, food, or even water. How long will this person hold up?

One who takes time for "selfish" acts of rest, food, and water—plus a little recreation—will be of much greater service over a longer period of time than one who "sacrifices everything" for others.

Once our primary needs—and a few fundamental wants—are met, the rest is overflow.

It is from this overflow that we give. It is simply what those who are natural givers do. Givers need to give. After the basic needs of life are met, givers enjoy giving more than they enjoy receiving.

What, to a taker, would be a sacrifice, to a giver, is a privilege.

TAKING CARE OF OURSELVES
VERSUS INDULGING OURSELVES

If we do more with less,
our resources will be adequate to take care of everybody.

BUCKMINSTER FULLER

Givers want to give. Our Western culture, however, encourages us more to get than to give.

Yes, our society pays a certain amount of lip service to giving, but most of our cultural messages involve the joys, satisfactions, and importance of obtaining, consuming, getting more. If we had a national cheer, it would probably be "More! More! More!"

The United States has 5% of the world's population yet consumes approximately 70% of the world's resources. (We also produce an inordinate amount of the world's pollution.)

Let's face it: we are a nation of gluttons—and we are often encouraged to believe this gluttony is good. That, however, is changing. That change has come from outside of us. Now it is time to make the inner change. To realize that giving is the higher path.

Some givers say, "I'll make more; then I'll give of the overflow." Some "givers" have been saying this for years. Some "givers" have made more, and rather than giving, they fell into the cultural trap of glamour and the overflow that was going to be used for giving was used to fill their swimming pools.

Perhaps the answer is to live more simply and give of the overflow we already have. This will make you a giver— and the Universe tends to give to true givers.

LEARN TO RECEIVE

Drop your feeling of resistance when the Universe
gives you more than you think you deserve.
That's what the Universe does—
it gives us more than we could ever deserve.
Open your arms wider and take it all in!

LAURA TERESA MARQUEZ

True givers receive in strange ways. By "true givers," I mean people who are actually physically involved in an ongoing process of giving; people who are not just committed to giving as an idea or concept, but people who actually give.

True givers know that they are merely caretakers— nothing more than warehousers and distributors of life's stuff. Stuff comes in; they find a need for it; stuff goes out. Stuff in; stuff out.

When the Universe (God, Mother Nature, the Tooth Fairy—whomever or whatever you see as the benevolent, giving force) wants to give to those who need, to whom do you suppose the Universe chooses to distribute these gifts? The givers, of course: the true givers.

So, if you're a true giver, learn to receive. Receiving can be one of the most challenging things for a giver to do.

When you are open to receive, things will come to you in the most amazing, unexpected ways. Don't evaluate whether you need them or not; receive them with gratitude on behalf of those to whom you will eventually give them (or, more accurately, pass them along).

Give, truly give, and a job giving to others will eventually be given to you. Don't pursue the job; pursue the service, and the job will pursue you.

SERVER, HEAL THYSELF

*There is no human problem which could not be
solved if people would simply do as I advise.*

GORE VIDAL

Whenever we have the desire to "fix" or change someone
in the name of service, perhaps it's good to remember the
age old proverb, "Physician, heal yourself!" [LUKE 4:23]

It's fine to serve, of course—to nurture, to care for, to
support, even to offer good advice when asked or when
another is clearly open to it.

When, however, we feel an overwhelming need to give
another an invaluable gem of our wisdom, which they seem
completely disinterested in hearing, much less following,
then perhaps it's time to heal ourselves.

What if that person is serving us by holding up a mirror
and reflecting back to us one of our own weaknesses?

That golden nugget of wisdom he or she so foolishly
disregarded need not go to waste, it can be used after all:
on us. We can find the relevance of that sage advice for
ourselves, and apply it.

There's no need to be perfect before we start giving; there
are plenty of people who are right now waiting for what
we have to give in the way we already know to give it. In
order to help more people at a higher level, however, we
must grow to a higher level ourselves.

And what's one of the best ways for givers to grow?
Through service, of course.

THROUGH SERVICE, OF COURSE

If you want to lift yourself up, lift up someone else.

BOOKER T. WASHINGTON

Whether we want to grow to new and dynamic levels of experience and expression, or whether we want to keep ourselves from going crazy*, service can be a most valuable vehicle.

The noted psychiatrist Karl Menninger was asked what he would recommend if someone felt a nervous breakdown coming on. He advised, "Find someone in need and do something for him."

Our physical health may depend upon giving as well. In study after study, those who regularly give are healthier, happier, and live longer than those primarily involved in getting.

If you're one of those people who doesn't live to give, then give to live.

One definition of "crazy" is doing the same thing over and over again expecting a different result.

THE WAY TO LEADERSHIP IS TO BE THE SERVANT

Give love and unconditional acceptance to
those you encounter, and notice what happens.

WAYNE DYER

Service to humanity has got to start with serving you. Start right here, right now, to serve yourself in the best way possible.

The way to leadership is to be the servant. That means to serve unconditionally. Learn to serve unconditionally, and you will be leading automatically.

Everybody around will feel, "This person can do it." "Can do" is the ability to do.

So if you're serving other people and you're not serving yourself, you're really not serving them. Because all of a sudden the resentment from your not feeling that you're getting yours will start to carry over to the next time you serve.

Pretty soon you're serving out of upset, and you are calling it service and love. You serve out of negativity when you say "I'd only work here for money." A lot of people do things for money they won't do for any other reason. That's why money is the king in this world.

Be of service to yourself by filling yourself up with your Spirit and your love. Then you don't need to overfill yourself with food because there's no place for it to go. You eat it for sustenance instead of for satisfaction.

Stay focused on what you're truly after. The mind wants to wander. So you have to bring the mind into service to you. Let it feed on what you want to feed it. Don't let it select the food.

WHEN WE GIVE TO SOMETHING GREATER THAN OURSELVES, WE BECOME GREATER TOO

The sage does not accumulate for himself.
The more he uses for others, the more he has himself.
The more he gives to others,
the more he possesses of his own.

LAO-TZU

Sometimes, something "bad" happens to us that doesn't seem to apply to our lives at all; whatever lessons might be gained don't seem to be directly applicable to our lives. Then, weeks, months, sometimes years later, someone will come along with precisely that problem, and we not only understand it, but we also have compassion for it—and, often, a solution. At those points, we realize we didn't go through the experience for us; we went through the experience for the other person.

So, in times of difficulty, ask not only, "How can I help myself out of this," but also, "How can I use this to help others?"

Service school is always in session.

When we give to someone, something, or some cause greater than ourselves, we feel transcendent and expanded. The person, thing, or cause we give to becomes greater for our gift, and, seemingly violating the law of physics, we become greater too.

This happens because giving does not follow the law of physics; giving follows the law of service. In service, all good is multiplied.

Adding our gift to something greater than ourselves multiplies the good for all.

GIVE QUIZ

If things are not going well with you,
begin your effort at correcting the situation
by carefully examining the service you are rendering,
and especially the spirit in which you are rendering it.

ROGER BABSON

Which are the magic words that transform a heartless exchange into heartfelt service?

a) *Alacazam*

b) *Attitude*

c) *Abracadabra*

d) *Altitude*

Answer: Attitude and Altitude. If the other ones work, by all means use them. Let's take a closer look at attitude and altitude.

ATTITUDE

Let's explore a fairly typical entry-level work situation: bagging burgers at the back of the local burger emporium. You may not see the people you serve. You may not even know how many people you serve: for every hundred burgers you wrap, you may have fed a hundred schoolchildren or two very hungry tourists. This is the type of work that can be a job or a joy depending upon your (ta da!) attitude.

The extremes in attitude the burger wrapper (the person, not the paper) could take:

"I'm so pleased I can help provide nourishment for my fellow human beings and do the best possible job I can for my boss."

Or:

"Damn wrappers, damn customers, damn burgers, damn boss, damn job, damn life."

Somewhere between *Pollyanna in Burgerland* and *The Burgerwrappers of the Damned* lies the range of attitudes that can make precisely the same activity either heartfelt service or heart-burdening servitude.

If your work is work to you, and you don't see beyond that work to see the joy and value in work and the joy and value in service, look out; you are in danger of standing in your present station for a long, long time.

Wrapping burgers with the conscious knowledge that you are making a contribution opens the heart. Counting the hours and cursing each burger closes the heart. It's a matter of attitude, and attitude is a matter of choice.

It certainly may not seem as though attitude is a matter of choice: our reactions seem so automatic. Depending on our conditioning and our body born conditions (genetics), life may appear either as a rose bush with thorns or a thorn bush with roses. Whether we focus on roses or thorns, however, is a choice.

With practice, we can recognize the programming earlier and earlier and challenge its seemingly inevitable results.

In time, a burger wrapper can watch the order for an extra hundred burgers come in and make a conscious choice: "Do I wrap these burgers with the attitude of heartfelt service or do I wrap these burgers with the attitude of heart-burdening servitude?" The choice will always be respected.

Eventually, we can reprogram ourselves to automatically see each request of our time, energy, or talents as an opportunity to serve. We may not be able to honor all requests, but those that we do can be done with a loving heart.

ALTITUDE

*From a distance the earth looks blue and green
and the snow-capped mountains white.*

*From a distance the ocean meets the stream
and the eagle takes to flight.*

*From a distance there is harmony
and it echoes through the land.*

*It's the voice of hope. It's the voice of peace.
It's the voice of every man.*

JULIE GOLD

In the 1960s, there was a Rocky and Bullwinkle cartoon in which Bullwinkle Moose launches Rocky, the flying squirrel, into the air. Rocky, soaring at cloud-level, looks down on the situation that formerly seemed perplexing.

"I see it all now!" exclaims Rocky.

"Well, you should, Rock," says Bullwinkle, "you're high enough."

That's what altitude does for us: it puts everything in perspective. As the Rocky part of us soars above and "sees it all now," the Bullwinkle part of us remains earth-bound, walking through life.

When we get "above it all" through meditation, contemplation, inspiration (reading, listening to tapes and lectures, taking workshops, counseling), or other uplifting activities, we can view life as nothing but opportunities to serve.

SERVICE IS BECOMING

Our deeds determine us,
as much as we determine our deeds.

GEORGE ELLIOTT

Ultimately, it's not a matter of what we receive from giving, but what we become by giving that matters.

Joy is a process of service. Are you serving?

Saying that you want to serve more is qualifying and conditioning what you do. "I want to serve more" means I'm not serving as much. And, if I'm not serving as much, that means I've got boundaries and conditions around it. That's conditional service.

If you say that you just really want to be more available and open to Spirit, those are nice words, but you just did a fairy tale. What does that mean and look and feel like and act like? How would we see you doing that?

Unbounded service is unbounded supply of energy and resource. Unbounded means you can never be tired until you say, "I'm tired." And then you've conditioned your energy.

Instead, say, "This is God's energy going through me, and there's infinite supply." Then keep facing into the infinite supply with God as your partner, and just keep moving it.

Does it mean you go faster and do more? No, no. It means that inside of you there's more of the fullness of the Spirit moving through you, and you have less and less to do except to be there as the Spirit comes through and serves and does all the miracles.

A very important place to start is to be loving with yourself.

47

HAVE FUN AND REJOICE IN IT

*The only service a friend can really render is to
keep up your courage by holding up to you a mirror
in which you can see a noble image of yourself.*

GEORGE BERNARD SHAW

Being of service is the most fundamental, direct, accurate, fast way to feel good about yourself. Do you think I have given over 6,000 seminars for you? Forget it. I do this for me.

I am of service because of what it gives to me, and what it takes away and relieves from me. I've just got to come and be of service and serve. And I do it willingly, giving it freely. I do not have to be accurate in what I say. I don't have to be right. I just have to be willing to be of service.

I used to do a lot of counseling. I'd go out in the waiting room to see how many people were still waiting to see me. There was always somebody else coming in. So I reached the place where I wouldn't go out there and look. I'd just say, "Next." Get the next one, get the next one, get the next one. And finally, at some point, somebody would lock the door so nobody could come in. I had finished.

I was always just doing one—the one in front of me. I never did do ten before the one in front of me and five more. I was always doing one. The one right here, right now.

That one was always new and fresh because it was one. But if it was like seven or eight, then my consciousness would immediately start comparing and running overwhelm on me and tiredness, and "I've done too much," and "What do they expect," and "What do they want?"

As long as you keep it to the one—this one—this is the day that the Lord has made, you then have your fun and rejoice in it.

THE SELFISHNESS OF SERVING

Start where you are. Distant fields always look
greener, but opportunity lies right where you are.
Take advantage of every opportunity of service.

ROBERT COLLIER

It is a paradox, but service must be done selfishly in order to be done in a selfless way; because if you don't take care of yourself, you can't take care of others.

So we have three groundrules we go by, mentioned earlier:
Take care of yourself so you can help take care of others.
Don't hurt yourself and don't hurt others.
Use everything for your upliftment, learning, and growth.

They are the three premises upon which we serve.

If you are not taking care of yourself, you are certainly not going to be able to take care of anybody else in a sustainable way.

I can be of better service to everyone if I'm a little more selfish in taking care of myself. Then I'm going to be of greater service than I would be ordinarily— because ordinarily I'd just cancel everything because of tiredness or exhaustion.

Your ability and willingness to serve other people helps keep you growing and opening so you get a great opportunity to uplift yourself. If that's your approach, I think you're absolutely on target. I think we are on target when we start to help each other to grow and to serve.

I say that serving is such a selfish thing because unconditional service is the highest form of consciousness on the planet. The more you serve, the higher your consciousness goes. The more you serve to get the higher consciousness, the further it goes down. It's just one of these things that has to be authentic and unconditional. And I would add that God loves a joyful giver.

GIVING IS SUCH A SELFISH THING

The giving of money, time, support, and encouragement to worthy causes can never be detrimental to the giver. The laws of nature are structured so that acts of charity will open an individual to an unbounded reservoir of riches.

JEFFREY MOSES

As we finish this section on giving to ourselves, allow me to mention again that the primary benefit givers get from giving is the joy of giving itself.

Giving is such a selfish thing.

I think the greatest joy from my perspective is being of service to your fellow man. When one person starts to touch into their aliveness and is of service, I don't know quite how to put it into words—something wonderful happens in their immediate environment. They start to transform the environment. That would be how I would say it and that still doesn't capture it.

Something magical happens.

PART THREE
Serving and Giving Others

" You cannot do a kindness too soon, for you
never know how soon it will be too late. "

RALPH WALDO EMERSON

THE DILEMMA OF GIVING TO OTHERS

The first great gift we can bestow
on others is a good example.

THOMAS MORELL

Giving to others has certain built-in problems. It seems to bring out the best, and the worst, in people.

What can be regarded by the giver as a good deed can be perceived by the receiver as meddling and do-gooding.

In giving to others, here are just a few of the dilemmas:

- *How can we possibly know what another truly needs, how can we presume to think that we have what it takes to fill that need, and how can we possibly not try?*

- *In giving to others, are we supporting them or supporting their weaknesses?*

- *Does this situation need the caring of an amateur or the skill of a professional?*

- *How do we know whether we're helping or interfering, putting an end to pain or cutting short a necessary process.*

- *How can we tell if we're being courageous or merely stupid?*

And, all of this is in addition to our own *personal* fear, guilt, hurt feelings, anger, and unworthiness that naturally arise in any new situation.

We'll explore some of these points as we go along. I do not plan to offer pat answers: your answers are already inside of you. I do plan to offer enough questions, techniques, and *possible* answers, from many points of view, for you to discover your own answers.

For now, I have two suggestions for you to ponder:

> *1. When giving to others, use your heart and your head.*
>
> *2. To the degree you can, don't confuse your emotions with your intuition.*

This is part of taking care of yourself.

BE PRACTICAL IN YOUR SERVICE

Noble deeds are most estimable when hidden.

BLAISE PASCAL

Many spiritual and religious teachings say to sacrifice yourself in order to give to others. Many religious groups get people to participate through coercion, or guilt, or a promise of something.

My perspective is that it's best to serve out of the good feeling you get for doing good because good is the right thing to do. And you can lovingly help your fellow humans without crippling them.

For example, when someone has a broken leg, they may need a crutch for awhile. Then you assist them to get therapy so they can get rid of the crutch and get going.

I'm one of these people who say, "You need a crutch? Use a crutch. If you need a cane, then use a cane. If you need a wheelchair—use it." Just don't be foolish about anything. Get up as fast as you can. Don't become dependent on it if you don't need to.

THE HEART WANTS TO SERVE

People who concentrate on giving good service always get more personal satisfaction as well as better business.

PATRICIA FRIPP

It's so important that we let people know we're there for them. For example, if you walk into a store and you can't find someone to assist you, there is a good chance you'll walk out. Not because they were rude—they weren't anything—but they weren't there for you.

If you do finally find someone, and they begrudgingly tell you what you need to know, you may say, "Oh, that's not quite what I had in mind," and walk out—because they weren't there for you.

When people give you information, and they're not present in their heart, you don't believe what they tell you. It's really important that we get that heart connection, which is beyond the intellect. In fact, it disrespects the intellect because, while you're saying that you will never do something again, your heart's got you doing it.

Why is the heart getting me to do something I say I'll never do again?

Because the heart wants to serve.

WHAT CAN ONE PERSON DO?

Every human mind feels pleasure
in doing good to another.

THOMAS JEFFERSON

What can one person do to make a difference in this world, to make a positive impact?

Some people say it is about having money or connections.

To me, we can make a positive difference living in our own personal integrity. Being true to oneself is the heart of personal integrity.

Being true to oneself requires commitment, awareness, courage, and practice. Consistently exercising our own integrity produces inner harmony—ultimately, extending the spirit of universal cooperation as more and more individuals choose to demonstrate their own integrity.

Living your integrity becomes the rule instead of the exception. It transforms the duality of your life. You may then observe its transformational currents radiating in wider and wider circles through your universe, and you become living proof that loving is not some abstract ideal but a very effective and practical way to live your life.

The greatest commandments are to love God and to love your neighbor as yourself. All the rest of the Bible is a commentary on how to do that. Sometimes you say, "I love my neighbor," but you won't help him push his car out of the ditch. Love is a nice idea, but it doesn't live unless it is manifested through loving and service.

Loving, serving, and working together we can redirect the potentially destructive course charted for our planet towards positive upliftment, where humanity wins. Don't wait for a better future. Create it now.

Everyone, at their essence, is spiritual, and we cannot judge their spirituality by what their physical body does. But I think all people that demonstrate spirituality have in common a loving, caring, sharing and serving, that underpins all they do no matter what they're doing.

You just may see them demonstrate it by a subtle loving touch to someone in need or a smile when they walk down the street.

Service can be such a simple thing and when done with a pure heart can bring a profound change to the one being served.

HAVING THE ENERGY TO DO

If I have been of service, if I have glimpsed more of the nature and essence of ultimate good, if I am inspired to reach wider horizons of thought and action, if I am at peace with myself, it has been a successful day.

ALEX NOBLE

Oftentimes, our concern is not that we might get sick, but that we won't have the energy to do what we want to do. With that thought, we feel too tired and we sit and let the television entertain us, or books or magazines.

That's why I tell you to do volunteer work for an organization. When you are serving people, it pulls the energy in line and a new direction appears.

SERVING LIKE WE BREATHE

And as we let our own light shine, we unconsciously give other people permission to do the same. As we are liberated from our fear, our presence automatically liberates others.

MARIANNE WILLIAMSON

One who truly serves, serves and deals with life in a natural, relaxed way.

People will be aware of that quality emanating from you. A spiritual warrior holding the attitude of unconditional service can, by walking into a room, disarm people from their negative thoughts and their animosities, by the nature of their calmness and peacefulness.

The warrior ability gives us the strength to walk into a room where there is disharmony. We don't turn away from any disharmony. We can enter into a conflict but not in conflict. We observe the conflict neutrally and bring our Light to the situation.

Regardless of the outcome, one who truly serves always maintains harmony within themselves.

We don't stand up and fight in the name of peace. We become peace.

RECEIVING

Pleasant words are a honeycomb,
sweet to the soul and healing to the bones.

PROVERBS 16:24

Receiving can be very difficult for some people. A lot of times people are not ready to receive a compliment, or even a kind comment.

It takes training to be able to give to someone in such a way that they don't feel like they're being looked down upon, belittled, or being told that they're not worthwhile.

When the giving is done from a heartfelt place of service, I have never yet found anyone who hasn't been grateful. In their gratefulness, they sent back to me a tremendous sense of loving that I wasn't expecting to receive.

I can't say my giving was always purely unconditional, but it was in that direction and with that intent. My attitude is, "I give this freely to you. Do with it as you want to, because it's in your hands."

EXPECTATIONS

All worthwhile men have good thoughts,
good ideas and good intentions—
but precious few of them ever translate those into action.

JOHN HANCOCK FIELD

A lot of times we give and we expect something in return. A while back, I remember giving someone a gift, and they turned around and gave it to someone else. At first it shook me up a little bit. Then I realized I needed to let go— to give without attachment. I realized that if the person wanted to give it to somebody else, well, hey, great!

I had to learn to give from beyond my ego. And the very process of doing that taught me what to do, because I had to access a place beyond the ego.

I learned that I could use the ego, but the source of inspiration is beyond the ego. I call it the spiritual heart. It's an endless source of energy and direction and enthusiasm.

The spiritual heart doesn't say, "Accomplish this big thing." It says, "Do these things so you can have more joy and have it more abundantly."

When I have shared this with people, they too have started coming more from the place of service rather than the place of ego, which always wants to get recognized for what it does. They have given and served from this heartfelt place and said that they would not have believed that it could feel so good giving in this way.

EVERYONE CAN GIVE A SMILE

Happiness, grief, gaiety, sadness, are by nature contagious. Bring your health and your strength to the weak and sickly, and so you will be of use to them. Give them not your weakness, but your energy, so you will revive and lift them up. Life alone can rekindle life.

HENRI-FREDERIC AMIEL

You may be reading this and saying, "What do I have to give?"

I think one of the greatest things we have to give is just to accept other people for who they are and not judge them or put them down.

Each of us can give a smile. Each of us can simply accept someone without looking down on them and criticizing them.

This is a gift that everyone can give, whether they have the financial means or not. Everyone has a heart and everyone knows how to smile, and everyone knows how to just accept people.

Even those who don't have much practice in how to accept others can just come to a place of, "Hey, you know, it's okay."

Maybe you don't agree with how someone lives their life, maybe you wouldn't do things the same way that they do, but you can still give them the acceptance of just saying, "It's okay. You have the right to be who you are in the moment."

That's something we can all give and it doesn't cost anything. We can all give just a moment where we are not imposing our way of being on someone else.

IT'S OKAY TO MAKE MISTAKES

Let him that desires to see others happy make haste to give while his gift can be enjoyed. He who waits to do a great deal of good at once will never do anything.

SAMUEL JOHNSON

Many people do not realize that this life is set up for us to make mistakes and to learn. I've learned a lot from my mistakes, and from people pointing out my mistakes.

Of course, I didn't like it.

But, when I stepped back, I thought, "No, I'll change this, because it's going to be easier to do now than if I get so ego-invested in it that I'll start fighting it. Then I'm going to judge those people and be negative towards them, and we know that energy follows thought, and so if I think negative, I'll start feeling negative and I'll start doing negative towards them. So, I have to stop this thing right at the very beginning."

Honor that voice within that tells you the best thing for you to do. Because, when you don't, you really get into a place of self-betrayal, and you may begin to slowly die inside. If you don't love yourself, you can easily close off to receiving all the good that is there for you to have. It's so important for you to follow your heart and to honor that voice that says, "Yes! Give to this person."

Whether it's a loving gesture, a smile, money, time, whatever it is, follow what your heart is saying. It comes right back to courage. Have the strength to follow your heart.

Everything in this life is a lesson. We learn, and we make mistakes. I have found out that giving is both the easiest and the most difficult thing that I'll ever have to do.

I think if we're willing to be a little foolish, a little playful, and just go and act on whatever giving thought comes to us—in other words, giving without getting into all the mind stuff—I think we could make the world such a better place.

If we really followed the direction straight from our spiritual heart, and just did these little things that, from the mind, we might judge—just let loose and do it anyway—a lot of us would find that our lives would be so much better and filled with joy.

GIVE BECAUSE IT IS IN YOU TO GIVE

Don't be selfish. If you have something you do not want, and know someone who has a use for it, give. In this way you can be generous without expenditure of self-denial and also help another to be the same.

ELBERT HUBBARD

It doesn't matter in my mind *who* says the truth—that it is said is what matters.

When you're being of real service, your joy surfaces, and it's fun, and it can even appear foolish. You may enjoy it so much you start to look for other reasons to be foolish and serve. I use the word childlike, rather than childish, to describe it.

The person being served gets the joy and the simplicity of it, and it by-passes all of their ego defenses, and that joy and childlike quality is in them, loving them, before they know it.

Maybe a big lesson for everyone is to give, not because you feel you have to, but because it's something you want to do, out of the joy that is in you.

Sometimes we take the position that we will only give to the person if they have the right and proper attitude. But if they had the right and proper attitude, they probably wouldn't be in the place to receive service from us.

So give from a place of unconditionality.

You give because it's in you to give.

WHAT DO WE GIVE?

Give what you have.
To someone, it may be better than you dare think.

HENRY WADSWORTH LONGFELLOW

What have you got? Talent? Kindness? Love? Patience?

Are you a good listener? Can you cook? Paint? Balance books? Make little horses out of pipe cleaners? Sing? Clean toilets?

Do you happen to know the president's (any president's) private phone number? Does he or she owe you a favor?

Do you know how to play "Chopsticks"? Use chopsticks? Make chopsticks?

Do you have the use of a car? Storefront? Lecture hall? Barn? Warehouse? Forty acres in the great white North? A bicycle?

Whatever you've got can be a real gift to others.

There was a member of a church congregation who complained about *everything*, but he also volunteered for everything. The volunteering was appreciated, but the complaining was driving everyone nuts.

Eventually, the pastor discovered the place to use this complaining volunteer best: he put the congregant in charge of complaining for the church. Any difficulty that the church had with the city, suppliers, repair people, or any other professional disputes were turned over to this one-person Bureau of Dispute Resolution to handle. It worked brilliantly.

Sometimes giving is creatively finding a useful outlet for the gift.

Somebody is waiting for that something you have to give.

MAKE YOUR OWN GIFT—
SUCH AS MONEY

*Money-giving is a very good criterion
of a person's mental health.
Generous people are rarely mentally ill people.*

KARL A. MENNINGER

Money is simply a *symbol of energy.* We trade an item, idea, or activity for a symbol of its value—money. We then exchange that symbol of energy (money) for another item, idea, or activity that we consider valuable.

Because money represents our energy, it can be looked at as an extension of ourselves.

Money represents a personal investment on our part—a symbol of our work, energy, ideas, or good fortune. As such, when we give money we are giving of ourselves.

So when someone says, "Oh, they only give *money,* they don't give of *themselves,*" they are usually making a mistake. Of course, love, affection, tenderness, and simply *being there* are essential to service. But money does have its place.

After all, in any service project *someone* is paying for the food, tools, transportation, office space, printing, telephones, accommodations, aspirin, and all the other goods and services necessary for service.

Money is sometimes as important to the act of giving as the love that inspires the act.

THERE IS NO LIMIT TO THE GOOD YOU CAN DO IF YOU DON'T CARE WHO GETS THE CREDIT

Riches may enable us to confer favors,
but to confer them with propriety and grace
requires a something that riches cannot give.

CHARLES CALEB COLTON

As I have pointed out before, we primarily give because it feels good to give. The recipient is but an innocent bystander.

Yet there is also a selfless dimension to service: giving with no thought of credit, reward, or appreciation from the recipient or the world at large.

Part of the fun of giving is doing it anonymously. Like the Lone Ranger, who never waited around to be thanked, leaving the grateful townspeople to ponder, "Who was that masked man?" I prefer to do good, disappear, and leave people wondering, "Who was that loving, crazy fool?"

"Hi-ho service, away!"

A PUBLIC DISPLAY ISN'T ALWAYS BAD

We should give as we would receive, cheerfully, quickly, and without hesitation; for there is no grace in a benefit that sticks to the fingers.

SENECA

Sometimes making a public display of giving inspires (or shames) others into giving too. Not everyone who donates publicly, then, is in it for the glory; many organizations find that well publicized gifts, especially from famous people, encourage gifts from others.

Elizabeth Taylor, for example, didn't have to do another thing for her name to be preserved in film history. Nevertheless, she decided in the mid-1980s, long before it became popular or even acceptable, to support research in finding the cure for AIDS and to provide care (and caring) for people with AIDS. She took a risk and put her fame, money, and prestige on the line because she wanted to serve.

Similarly, Mary Tyler Moore, who is among the richest women in show business (according to *Fortune*), still does a great many public appearances, which she would never do merely for money. She is the spokesperson for the Juvenile Diabetes Foundation and, as such, she makes appearances in that capacity as an expression of her giving.

Jerry Lewis has famously raised money for Multiple Sclerosis for years.

There are many ways to give and serve.

BE KIND TO UNKIND PEOPLE— THEY MAY NEED IT MOST

Don't use the impudence of a beggar
as an excuse for not helping him.

RABBI SCHMELKE

Some people spend an inordinate amount of time and energy making sure that the recipients of their gifts are *truly* deserving and have the *right attitude*.

Frankly, if they had the *right attitude*, they probably wouldn't need your gift.

You'll find that giving freely is a lot more fun. The heart is so much bigger than the mind.

Certainly one of the reasons givers wish to ease other's difficulties is because there is already entirely too much pain in the world.

This is not an easy life.

Those with feelings can feel the pain in their own lives; those with compassion can feel the pain in others' lives. Those who feel this pain, this darkness, have no desire to add to the darkness.

Givers by their nature want to ease burdens, lighten loads, and spread Light.

LISTEN

The love of our neighbor in all its fullness simply means being able to say to him, "What are you going through?"

SIMONE WEIL

Sometimes the greatest gift is not saying a word. Ten minutes of active, compassionate, nonjudgmental listening can often do more than several hours of dispensing "good advice."

When others know that when they talk to us there is a "safe space" in which they can say anything they want without thought of reprisal, condemnation, or fear of having a confidence betrayed, they not only find comfort in being able to speak about their difficulty but often find their own solutions as well.

Givers, being compassionate, are often more aware of suffering in this world. The people who create the suffering are usually quite unaware that they are doing so. "Unconscious" seems to be the term that best describes these people.

The challenge for givers, in a world that seems bent on destruction and pain, is to keep giving anyway.

It is worth the effort. A single candle can overcome a lot of darkness.

THE GIFT OF HEALING

*In the sick room, ten cents' worth of
human understanding equals ten dollars'
worth of medical science.*

MARTIN H. FISCHER

Some know they have the gift of healing; some are not so sure; others deny it.

If you're a true giver, if you put your body on the line in the name of giving, you are a healer.

By taking your compassion, warmth, Light, and love to those who need physical, emotional, mental, or spiritual healing, you help healing to take place.

Oh, your visit (or call or card or sending the Light) may not bring about an instantaneous, complete healing, but a lot more healing happened because you directed your time and intention towards healing.

There is no need to concern yourself with the "hows" of healing—just go give. Take the Light with you and use it for the highest good, and healing will happen, for the highest good.

YOU GIVE WHAT YOU GIVE;
THEY GET WHAT THEY GET

I know what I have given you.
I do not know what you have received.

ANTONIO PORCHIA

Our giving can only go so far. At a certain point, it is up to the other person to receive. When we've given what we can, in the best way we know how, in line with our best intentions, we can only release the gift with the thought, "for the highest good of all concerned," and let it go.

From that point on, how the gift is received, what gift is received, or even if the gift is received at all, is all in the hands of another.

If it seems as though your service is not appreciated, let it go. You gave. Next time you can take your service elsewhere.

As givers, of course, it's not appreciation we seek; but if absolutely no appreciation is forthcoming, perhaps our gifts would do more good if given elsewhere.

KEEP IT GOLDEN

Do not do unto others as you would that they should do unto you. Their tastes may not be the same.

GEORGE BERNARD SHAW

When Jesus presented what is generally known as the Golden Rule by stating, "So in everything, do to others what you would have them do to you," [MATTHEW 7:12] it had been ancient wisdom more than five centuries earlier when Confucius said, "What you do not want done to yourself do not do to others."

This ancient wisdom is often misinterpreted as, "The things I like having done to me, I should do to others." Or, put more plainly, "What's good for me must be good for everybody—whether they like it or not."

Just as we want to be "done to" in ways that we can enjoy, accept, and value, so, too, we must give to others in ways that *they can* enjoy accept, and value.

Certainly, there's no need to compromise our *principles*; it's just that sometimes when giving, we must set aside our *preferences* and keep the highest good of the other person in mind.

THE TIES THAT BIND

Perhaps the greatest social service that can be rendered by anybody to this country and to mankind is to bring up a family.

GEORGE BERNARD SHAW

For some, loving their spouse and raising good children is the highest possible service.

Heaven knows, being even marginally successful at these goals is service enough for a lifetime.

If you have taken on the monumental task of supporting a spouse and raising a family, you need never look outside the home to be of ongoing, continuous, and, one might add, exhaustive service.

Often good spouses and good parents are the unsung heroes of our time.

MARRIAGE—A GREAT OPPORTUNITY FOR UNCONDITIONAL SERVICE

Home is the place where, when you have to go there, they have to take you in.

ROBERT FROST

Those of you who are married have probably been given one of the better opportunities to grow and be of unconditional service. When you come into that place of serving out of the reverence for the divinity in your spouse, disregarding their personality, habits, and any physical disability they may have, in the reverence of doing that, you might find a whole different type of person inside of you, one that doesn't have the karma still pushing on you.

It may be that splitting up with your husband or wife is a wonderful idea, and it could also be a very poor choice. You're not going to have their baggage to carry around, but you're still carrying around your own baggage because it's not being serviced out. So you could then create an alcoholic person, or a nut case, or a spendthrift to get married to.

You create that somebody to come into your field for you to serve them in order to fulfill and clear the karma.

You may be saying, "Well, great, and when do I get served?" The answer is after you finish up the karma. And you may ask, "When's the end of that?" The end is when the end appears.

If you keep thinking that you would do better in a sexually intimate relationship, what you need to do is realize that you don't go into a relationship for sexual needs.

You go into it for the spiritual attunement with another individual with whom you can start to share your life.

That sharing means that you serve them, and they serve you. It's an exchange. That way there's no such thing as divorce.

VOLUNTEERING

This is our special duty, that if anyone specially needs our help, we should give him such help to the utmost of our power.

CICERO

Serving others is a way of expressing gratitude and, in the process, receiving gratitude.

When we feel the bliss of that receiving, that is our spiritual nature giving back to us as a way of saying we are on track and that we are in harmony with what we have come into this life to do.

When we serve, a knowing, a loving, a greater awareness, and a whole lot of learning come forward.

If you are someone who works with volunteers, what do you think you could do to make their volunteering more enriching and nurturing? I can tell you that loving them is the top priority.

It's amazing how a little acknowledgment can go a long way. A simple handwritten note of thanks, for example, or a kind word can go a long way. These are loving actions because you are not saying just words of love but demonstrating you love them, and that you care.

THE HIGHEST SERVICE

When we grow old, there can only be one regret—
not to have given enough of ourselves.

ELEONORA DUSE

The highest form of service is unconditional. Even if I do something that you don't like, or you hear I do something you don't like, there's still no reason for you to withhold your loving and service to me. None. In unconditional service, we love and serve each other, regardless.

Service, primarily, is just being with a person in the most loving, caring way that you can. That does infer that you then take your desires, wants, needs, behaviors, and put them aside and serve according to the needs of the person in front of you.

There may be times when you say, "I don't know if I am serving or not." Just go ahead and serve anyway. Give yourself the benefit of the doubt.

If you love God and you serve your fellow man, God is faithful and true to his promise. But it is a spiritual promise, not a material world promise.

The flow of energy in giving and serving is so important. Whether in an intimate relationship or a business relationship, to be able to say, "Is there anything else I can do for you?" and mean it from your heart is a most wonderful thing.

DO IT!

All the beautiful sentiments in the world
weigh less than a single lovely action.

JAMES RUSSELL LOWELL

When it actually comes time to serve, we will be met by the limitations of the comfort zone. The comfort zone is all the activities we have done often enough that we feel comfortable doing them. When serving in a new area, in a new way, or with new people, we often feel uncomfortable. The feelings of discomfort are generally the emotions of fear, guilt, unworthiness, hurt, and anger.

We must be prepared to experience these feelings, and *physically move into service anyway.*

As we move into service, fear can become enthusiasm; guilt can become the energy to make changes within ourselves; unworthiness can remind us that no matter what, we are worthy to serve; hurt feelings can remind us of how much we care (underneath all hurt feelings is caring); and anger, properly directed, can become the energy to make a positive change.

Don't wait until you are perfect; don't wait for the perfect opportunity; don't wait for more to give; don't wait for a more deserving recipient; don't wait until you're more comfortable; *don't wait.*

Do it!

AND DO IT NOW!

The smallest good deed is better
than the grandest good intention.

JACQUES-JOSEPH DUGUET

If you have read this far in the book without taking our earlier suggestion—to put the book down often and go serve and give—this could be a great time to put the book down now and go serve and give.

If you're still reading and not doing, allow me to remind you of the story of the terribly timid giver who desperately wanted to do good for others but could never quite bring herself to do so.

Somehow, she always allowed her fear to be greater than her need to give. One day, however, she saw an unfortunate man standing on a street corner, and, moved by compassion, she summoned all her courage to scribble "Best of luck" on a $100 bill. She thrust it into the man's hand as she quickly passed by.

The next day, the man approached the woman, handed her $1,000, and said, "Nice work, lady. Best of Luck paid ten to one."

So, right now, before turning to the next section, feel free to go serve and give—even if it's just a phone call or a postcard.

Enjoy!

PART FOUR
Serving and Giving to God

" Man discovers his own wealth
when God comes to ask gifts of him. "

RABINDRANATH TAGORE

WHAT GOOD DO
YOU WANT TO DO?

We live very close together, so our prime purpose in this life is to help others. And if you can't help them, at least don't hurt them.

THE DALAI LAMA

Whatever your view of God, or by whatever name you call the divine energy that breathes us and sustains all life—giving to God and to all that God has created—can be among the most satisfying forms of service.

What do you want to give to? A good cause? Good government? Good works? Good organizations? Good earth? Good day?

We can, of course, give to all the goodness in life by sending Light to it. When it comes to investing time, money, or energy, however, we must choose carefully.

You can give of yourself physically to *any* good you want, but you cannot give to every *good* you want.

Serving another with loving, caring, and sharing is God doing unto God the godly things—sharing the blessings of health, wealth and happiness; abundance, prosperity and riches; loving, caring and sharing—but the really big thing is touching. Touching physically, emotionally, mentally, and spiritually. Touching. Not hanging on. Just the gentle blessing of touching.

Perhaps, ultimately, the only true good is God. So let's explore that a little more deeply in the following pages.

YOUR SPIRITUAL PROGRESSION

The greatest reward for serving others is the satisfaction found in your own heart. The roots of happiness grow deepest in the soil of service.

SAMSON R. HIRSCH

The action of Spirit is always one of service, of giving.

If you want to know where you are in your spiritual progression, look at your giving.

If you want to know where you are in your materiality, look at your receiving and what you do with it.

We grow physically by taking food, water, and air into our bodies.

We grow emotionally when we receive love, support, and encouragement, particularly when times are tough like when someone says lovingly to us, "Come on, stand up, I know you can do it." And we stand up and do it, and we grow, we mature.

We grow mentally by getting educated, taking in information, learning it, memorizing it, making it part of our character.

So, we grow physically, emotionally, and mentally by taking. However, we grow spiritually by giving.

You give mentally by sharing what you've learned with others. You give emotionally by loving and supporting people. You give physically by being of service and helping others. And, therefore, in this giving, you grow spiritually and know the Beloved in yourself and others.

No one else will have to tell you where you are in your spiritual progression. You can look at your life and decide that for yourself.

CHOOSE THIS DAY
WHOM YOU WILL SERVE

Great opportunities to help others seldom come,
but small ones surround us daily.

SALLY KOCH

You can serve your vanity, serve your judgments, or serve God who created you.

You're going to have to let go of feeling not beautiful enough, not talented enough, not worthy enough, because ordinariness is the prior condition to God—not beauty or talent or worthiness.

I don't choose whom you should serve. I only choose for me. As the Bible says, "Choose you this day whom you will serve... But as for me and my house, we will serve the Lord" [JOSHUA 24:15].

It's not a good or a bad; that's between you and God, and it's none of my business. It's your business.

Good gravy, just do the best you can as bad as it may look to you. Isn't doing our best truly all that we can do? So, just start, you'll get better as you go along.

THE MESSAGE OF THE CHRIST

One of the most amazing things ever said on this earth is Jesus' statement: "He that is greatest among you shall be your servant" [MATTHEW 23:11].

Nobody has one chance in a billion of being thought really great after a century has passed except those who have been the servants of all. That strange realist from Bethlehem knew that.

HARRY EMERSON FOSDICK

Christ is forgiving. He is for give-ing. Jesus said, "I come to serve you." Isn't serving, giving?

Why did Christ say to go and serve his people—to give this message to his people. What is the message?

God loves all of its creation.

Out of God come all things.

The mind that is in Christ Jesus is the same mind that can be in you because it's there ready to be awakened.

Awaken the positive faculties in you, and forgive everyone every action towards you—good or bad—and walk in that loving feeling of looking at people as though you have seen Christ also, in and through their flesh.

SERVING THE LORD IN EVERYONE YOU MEET

The fragrance always remains
in the hand that gives the rose.

HEDA BEJAR

We can dissolve most of our differences with amicable conversation.

And if we have to yell at each other to get through, okay, then let's yell; but when we get through, let's hug and laugh and break bread together.

Do those things that you know can heal wounds and animosities. It doesn't matter whether the other person accepts it or not. Do it for you. Then you are free.

It's also possible that years later they'll accept your loving gesture and then be thankful. You don't know what they can and cannot accept just now. But serve them now because it is free for you to do now.

Don't inflict by insisting that they must receive your service in a certain way or that you have to say the words a certain way. Just let your heart speak its truth, not *the* truth, *its* truth of loving and caring—without detailing out all the wrongs they did to you and why you're being gracious to them.

I think then you'll find that your life can really take on that essence where you say, "I'm serving the Lord in everybody I meet." That's going to be nice because you'll be in heaven, and you'll be walking on the earth.

SERVING MATERIALITY VERSUS SERVING THE LORD

What a man does for others, not what they do for him,
gives him immortality.

DANIEL WEBSTER

I wake up in the morning and I re-choose. I choose each day. And each day is called, "Choose you this day whom you will serve" [JOSHUA 24:15]. Do you serve Mammon, materiality, or do you serve the Lord?

Now, materiality is not necessarily money. Money is innocent, neutral—it's just a medium of exchange. And materiality isn't bad if used correctly. Materiality is physical things in life that can be used to serve the Lord. However, this planet has for too long been a place where materiality is the master and where human beings are of service to materiality. It's a downward path. Just look.

See, I have no conflict whatsoever with the materiality in my life. It is in service to my life purpose, and I place it with service so my life is going in one direction. It makes things easier, happier, and healthier, and it rarely gets boring.

If the Lord were to walk into the room now, how would we serve ourselves and the Lord and anybody who happened to be here? I think we would do it with awe, with reverence, with loving, with caring, and with making sure that everybody is okay. Not hurting, harming anybody. You see, it's a very easy relaxed place to be.

We can live our lives that way. It's effortless. The effort is in changing our conditioning and habits that say it is hard. You can serve with your next breath.

THE BIG PICTURE

I know of no great men except those who have
rendered great service to the human race.

VOLTAIRE

In the big picture there isn't a "leader," nor is there a "follower"—there are only those who serve.

God is a server, and a giver, and a doer. So, when we are authentically aligned and congruent with our true selves, we're serving and doing and sharing as a natural expression. In that state of consciousness, the loving and caring reaches out and touches others.

People will follow that quality in a person more than they will follow somebody who stands on a box and repeats beautiful sayings and poetry, or rattles off their educational credentials and says, "Come follow me."

Our response would be, "No, we're going to follow this person over here who hasn't said a word in twenty years; but when you're around them, you know that everything is in its place and that this person knows what's going on."

Do you get the idea how powerful the soul can be when its presence is allowed to shine even in the silence?

THE RESPONSIBILITY OF
HIGHER CONSCIOUSNESS

*Those who bring sunshine into the lives
of others cannot keep it from themselves.*

JAMES M. BARRIE

Some people want to have a higher consciousness so they can gain an advantage over other people.

But there is a responsibility that comes with having a higher consciousness, and it is that you must now start to serve people in this world. (I choose my words carefully and do not use "must" very often.)

That doesn't mean you have to go out and preach, or be evangelical or fanatical in your approach. Just be the spiritual being that you are.

As you move through the world, in that higher consciousness, those that need serving will call out to you. They're not going to call out to you when you feel like serving. They're going to call out in their timing and according to their need.

When you call for help, would you like God to answer you immediately? Or do you think God should do it on appointment schedules, or alphabetically—and your name starts with "Z"?

No, you'd rather that when you say, "Oh, God, help!" He responds with "I got ya!"

If that's how you want to be treated, that's how you need to be prepared to serve others, because it's done to you according to how you do it to others. If you serve with loving and caring, guess how it will be returned to you—with loving and caring.

SERVING IN GOD'S NAME

To give real service you must add something
which cannot be bought or measured with money,
and that is sincerity and integrity.

DOUGLAS ADAMS

God is here now, in this moment, and only sustains the present step.

If you're wondering whether you will have enough enthusiasm three weeks from now, I don't know. What are you going to be doing three weeks from now, sleeping all the time? You don't need enthusiasm while you're sleeping.

But when you get up to go, you can ask for that enthusiastic energy to assist you.

The way we do that is to do all things in God's name.

So in the morning we get up, we say, "Lord, in your name, and only in your name, do I do these things, and for You and what You have me to do for You. I'm here to serve You and Your people."

That is then doing things in God's name.

There may not be too much to do that day because most of His people aren't willing to move themselves actively to the place where it's to happen.

However, when they do, you will be ready to serve.

PLANTING LIGHT COLUMNS

Men are rich only as they give.
He who gives great service gets great rewards.

ELBERT HUBBARD

A few years ago, in New York City, a group of Light bearers would meet every other Sunday and place columns of Light at the openings of the subways and in the actual subways. And they would go to the parks, and they would place them there and have parties in the park afterward.

One of the last times I flew into New York, I looked out the window, and I said, "My, there's a tremendous fog over the city. There's this white mist all over Manhattan Island." Then I rubbed the window, and I sat back and looked again, and I realized that all of the Light columns placed all over that city were reaching miles above the city. And I could just see this mist of white Light all over, and I realized that it was the work of these Light bearers.

Sometimes they would go out in groups of four, and they would just place a Light column. How did they place a Light column? They'd close their eyes, and some of them would just imagine or envision a big white pillar of Light in front of them. And they would say a prayer to ask God to place the Light column there. Because we know we don't have the ability. But God does.

GOD'S WILL

I slept and dreamt that life was joy. I awoke and saw
that life was service. I acted and behold, service was joy.

RABINDRANATH TAGORE

We can serve from the place of the will of God by being in God's will.

God's will is loving all beings, being useful to all beings, and serving all beings without asking, "When do I get mine?"

You're getting yours by the action of serving. But if you're going to serve to get it, you will never get it because that's a negative approach of serving to get. The positive action is simply serving without conditions. Then the reward is naturally present within the action of serving because it comes out of that pure place.

We continually have the challenge of which reality of Spirit to live in. The reflected reality, which is Spirit in the natural world, or the unreflected reality that is unseen but is the real Spirit inside.

In the serving of others, from this unseen reality, you will grow and you will automatically serve yourself. You are sowing a field full of beautiful flowers because you've done good (God) works.

If you serve for recognition, to be seen, you are sowing weeds; they, too, grow automatically. Don't blame somebody else who's got the flowers. You may say that you did exactly the same thing that they did, and perhaps you did—physically, outwardly.

But inwardly you were corrupt because you served for recognition. You were negative inside and you judged, and nobody could tell by looking at your face because you smiled so beautifully and you acted so spiritual.

However, the Spirit inside of you is never fooled.

THE HIGHER ORDER OF SERVICE

The thing that lies at the foundation of positive change,
the way I see it, is service to a fellow human being.

LECH WALESA

It's easy to tell the difference between the lower order of service and the higher order of service.

The higher order has unity and usefulness and joy.

It's not that you say that you hear a higher order voice and you get to be of service. That's an ego trip.

Some people, who have gone on service projects to help people, have looked in the paper the next day to see if their names were mentioned. Others didn't care because they knew that if you get your reward out there, you don't get it where it counts—inside of you. It is inside where you have the joy of having been of service to the oneness in all of us.

There is a difference in people who are following the oneness on the upward path, because there's a bright Light that comes out of them. There is a truth that speaks through their voice. You hear something in their words— not the vocabulary they use, but in the energy of their words. It touches that place inside of you that is open to inspiration.

THE GREATEST THING WE CAN DO

One drop of water helps to swell the ocean; a spark of fire will help to give light to the world. None are too small, too feeble, too poor to be of service. Think of this and act.

HANNAH MORE

The greatest thing we can do here physically is to be—and I will use the word "total"—to be of total service to another.

This means you need to have totally served yourself first.

And if two hours of spiritual exercises or meditation does that, then you have done it. And if fifteen minutes does it, then you have done it.

DIVINE ORDINARINESS

*It is high time that the ideal of success
should be replaced by the ideal of service.*

ALBERT EINSTEIN

When we are in God's will, and we're following God's will, we are in a loving, caring place. We are being useful to other people and we are serving them. We have compassion and charity that emanate from us without our even knowing it.

Then people say, "My, you're so giving, and full of loving." You might reply, "I am? I didn't know that. I'm just being me. It's no big thing."

Somebody who isn't in touch with that divine ordinariness will not be as open. When somebody says that they really serve a lot, they'll reply, "Yeah, I'm real good at it." That's the ego creeping in, and it starts to lower the quality of the action.

It's one thing to neutrally and factually acknowledge that you do something, and another to claim it to boost your ego, saying in effect, "Look how great I am, look what I do for you, and you're so your lucky I am doing it."

WE ARE ALL PRODIGAL SONS

Happiness cannot come from without. It must come from within. It is not what we see and touch or that which others do for us which makes us happy; it is that which we think and feel and do, first for the other fellow and then for ourselves.

HELEN KELLER

We all are prodigal sons because we, many of us, feel as if we've been cast out of God's kingdom, and we want to return to it and be part of it.

When we are of service here in this world, that is actually better than being something, somewhere else; because when we're being the servant to each other, we are in the Father's house.

So when we are of service even when things are at their worst, we've got it really good. When we serve, our worst time is better than other people's best times. It's a cause for celebration, and dancing—celebrating the joy of living and sharing with each other. It's a deep emotional, terrific feeling. It touches very deeply. That's its nature. If you feel deeply, you're going to love deeply. You're going to be a person that when you move on something, people can count on it being moved on.

A lot of people who volunteer to do the work of Spirit do better than the people who are paid because they're doing it for the joy of serving and wanting to do it. The employees are often just doing it for the money. Do you understand that there's a real difference? There's a greater willingness in the volunteer to serve unconditionally in the "Father's house."

99

SERVING—A BRIDGE INTO GRACE

The life of man consists not in seeing visions
and in dreaming dreams, but in active charity
and in willing service.

HENRY WADSWORTH LONGFELLOW

If times get hard, there's no need to cry to God. There's only a need to have the grace of loving God. That loving starts to transmute and purify you once again as a prince and princess of the higher consciousness, and you start once again to come into that purple majesty and the royalty of your beingness.

And lest you be turned from that magnificence, you start serving the world because that serving solidifies the bridge into grace. You've heard me say that there is no higher consciousness on the planet than service. That doesn't necessarily mean scrubbing the floors. It means being with the person next to you for their upliftment, perhaps even silently.

SERVING MULTIDIMENSIONALLY

The purpose of life is to live a life of purpose.

ROBERT BYRNE

I do not want to be able to control what I am going towards. I want to work in such close cooperation with Spirit that it might look and seem that I am in control, but I'm not.

But it's also true that in that close cooperation with Spirit, there is so much oneness that perhaps I'd also say that I am in control, because I have now made It and me the same thing.

At that point, the Father and I are one. There's no difference. And at that point, what care I of others' opinions or what I am in control of or not, because I am in connection with the energy that is going back into the heart of God.

SEEING GOD

The highest exercise of charity
is charity towards the uncharitable.

J. S. BUCKMINSTER

Is it possible to see God? Absolutely. In fact, that happens to be the business that I'm in, telling people that there is a God, so that they can see God.

Of course, you may think you need to be a rare individual to be able to see God, but perhaps you don't need to be rare at all, just very ordinary.

Perhaps if you're loving and you're caring, you may see God in the loving and in the caring. When you are of service to other people, you may see God in the serving.

I know you can feel God in the joy that bubbles up inside when you have overcome something that has been distracting you from your purpose of life.

When that distraction is put in its proper place—not necessarily destroyed, but when the negativity of it is taken into the positive—what before was split is now whole. What was terrible before is now wonderful.

And nothing really changed except your attitude.

THE GLORY OF GOD

Prayer in action is love, and love in action is service. Try to give unconditionally whatever a person needs in the moment. The point is to do something, however small, and show you care through your actions by giving your time.

MOTHER TERESA

One day when it came to me that "Virtue is its own reward," I felt that it was the first time those words were ever spoken anywhere on the planet. I wanted to write them down and put my name on them, but then I found out that somebody else had said it, many years ago. But because it was new to me, it didn't matter. It was my discovery of that beautiful place inside that was Spirit-filled.

Then I realized that Spirit is its own reward. Happiness is its own reward. Loving is its own reward. The ability to serve is its own reward. The ability to give is its own reward. The ability to receive is its own reward.

Suddenly, it was really clear to me that it is inside of me where the whole makeup of creation resides. If I'm doing things to get a reward, to get recognition or delight from anyone out there in the world, I'm doing it *completely* backwards. So I started doing things for me, which I have found is the best approach. To love your neighbor as yourself carries the inference that you are to love yourself so that you *can* love your neighbor.

I realized it was also my responsibility to love the neighbor inside of me. That came in like a rush of wind from heaven. It was really a beautiful feeling to know and say, "Yes, there are many times I have missed the mark, but I'm in the glory of God."

Then it hit me—everybody is in the glory of God—everyone is in that.

WHERE TWO OR MORE
ARE GATHERED

He that returns a good for evil obtains the victory.

THOMAS FULLER.

It's not just that two or more are gathered "in my name." But can you imagine when the energy of being "in my name" moves into the focus of being loving? God can't stay away. You'll just pull the spirit of loving into the room through you.

We not only love each other, we honor each other and respect each other and allow the space of growth for each other. It's the sacredness of "Not my way, Lord, Your way."

When the Lord's way becomes your way, you can smile because you know you've got it, and you're on your way.

You see the face of God in everything around you.

The loving of seeing God is the loving that I teach.

EFFORTLESS SERVICE

Live simply that others may simply live.

ELIZABETH SEATON

It's one thing to be of service as a reward mechanism. "I'm of service, see, look at me, I'm of service." That's a reward mechanism.

It's another thing to be of service as a loving action that comes from the heart.

The Father-Mother God comes forward in you and actually starts to perform the action of your work and service through your being. You find it effortless. You experience it going better than you ever expected. And you find it ending sooner than you anticipated.

SERVING THE SPIRIT

Consciously or unconsciously, every one of us does render some service or other. If we cultivate the habit of doing this service deliberately, our desire for service will steadily grow stronger, and will make, not only our own happiness, but that of the world at large.

MAHATMA GANDHI

There's a statement in the Bible, that you can't serve God and Mammon [LUKE 16:13]. And Mammon can represent any of the things we put before God. This can include our doubt and our worry. So when these areas of contraction become the focus of your attention, it means you have taken the attention off God and placed it in the personality and material areas of this world—effectively, you are worshiping that.

All you have to do is say, "Okay, I've been in service to that, and I'm through with that form of service. Now I'm going to serve more of the higher vibration. I am going to serve Spirit."

There is no judgment in all this; we have all done similar things sometimes when there is a practical necessity to do it. When the car is running out of gas, we take it to the gas station and fill it. But an empty tank doesn't stay as a focal point in your mind. You fill the tank and then you no longer worry about running out of gas. It's done.

It's all in your attitude, not the mechanics of what you do. You serve the necessary things until they're complete and now you are free to serve the Spirit form. When the tank starts to go towards empty, you stop and serve it, and then you focus once again on serving the Spirit.

It's practical spirituality.

THE SACREDNESS OF SERVING

The simple act of helping someone—with no desire (or possibility) of repayment—is good for us and our self-image, and it may positively change the life or outlook of the receiver for the day!

KEVIN EIKENBERRY

You can dwell in the house of God forever because you're dwelling in the house now.

You just happen to be outside in the servants' quarters. But you can get in to the main house periodically.

If you're in the servants' quarters, there's an implication that you are there to be serving. That implication is having a willingness to serve and doing whatever is given to you to serve.

If this beautiful person, called your wife or your husband, is being given to you to serve, then why should you demand that they sit at some other table? Why are you not happy that serving in the Lord's house and feeding the anointed one is a blessing amplified beyond words?

Yes, you are blessed above all other people because you are being given that opportunity to serve from the sacred place of giving and loving.

You need to get your attitude right to truly dwell in the Lord's house.

It awaits you.

TAKING GOOD CARE OF YOURSELF

Joy can be real only if people look upon their life as a service and have a definite object in life outside themselves and their personal happiness.

LEO TOLSTOY

If you're depressed, down, or feeling negative, start taking good care of yourself to bring yourself out of what is confining and limiting and restricting you, so that you then have the freedom to be of service to others.

By shifting yourself out of the negative into the neutral or positive you have served yourself.

Most people use the concept of taking care of themselves as a way to feel self-pity or act in a spoiled way. They indulge their senses instead of freeing their senses to the service of God, which would then become their liberation.

So when negative things appear—like discouragement, unworthiness, or jealousy—you can say, "Well, here you are," and make peace with them, instead of judging them and judging yourself for judging them, and then suddenly you've locked yourself in prison. You educate the negative parts of yourself. You don't need to eradicate them. You love them, and then they will serve you.

You'll then realize that you're not in bondage to anything or anybody. You're at the service of the Lord. And the Lord may be moving you in ways that other people don't understand; so don't let people manipulate you into their way if that is not the direction you are going.

I've found out that in my work the more I serve, the more opportunity I have to serve, which is also more

108

opportunity to grow and to experience more of God's Light in everything. It's just a natural progression.

When I find a restriction or a confinement in me, in someone else, in the world, I do not look it at negatively. I look at it as something that I turn and face and see what it is.

I come to peace with it and then I move on again.

GOD IS MY PARTNER

Not the maker of plans and promises, but rather the one who offers faithful service in small matters. This is the person who is most likely to achieve what is good and lasting.

GOETHE

If I am working with God as my Partner, I would let people know my ability rests upon the honesty and the integrity of the Spirit of who I am and is my blessing.

I would stand forward as a person who does indeed believe in providence, divinity, God, Christ—whatever term the person I am speaking to relates to.

I wouldn't shy away from letting people know that that's who the Chairman of my Board is, and that I perform all my services under that spiritual direction, so that they would see the service that I do and the good that I do.

Where people might think that others only get ahead because they are dishonest, they'd see that I get ahead because I do good works. And that I do it through direction of Spirit—my Mentor in what I am doing.

My good works would then stand as the reference point to that. If people didn't want to believe that, then I would be working with other people anyway. I would allow them to have their own belief system. If they believed that I was a crooked guy, I guess they'd just have to be allowed to believe that as I continue doing good works.

I see no conflict, then, in doing things in the world and still questing God. I would just make God your Partner in all of your endeavors.

SERVING THE BELOVED

The great lesson to learn of life is the need of giving out from the abundance of one's self in order to be ever abundant within one's self.

WALTER RUSSELL

An example of unconditional service is when you volunteer your time and do what needs to be done, as though you were being paid but don't receive acknowledgement either in pay or thanks. In this way, you are serving for your Spirit—for the Beloved.

Then the ability to do gives you the ability to do more. You serve people with loving, caring, and sharing through your heart and into the world. As you do that, you feed yourself. If the food tastes bitter, then you didn't really serve. You portrayed service. It was, "Look at me. I'm cleaning the floors."

It would have been better for you to serve at night when no one was around to see you. Then when people come to work in the morning and see the floors clean and shiny, and do not know who did it, you get your recognition in the spirit.

When you get the recognition physically as in, "Oh, you did a wonderful job, that's so terrific," you've received what you're going to get out of that action. You got the praise of humans and that's not counted towards your soul. Yes, by all means, feel good about it, because that's all you're going to get out of it.

THE CHRIST ACTION
IN THE WORLD

We are all God's children so it is important to share His gifts. Do not worry about why problems exist in the world— just respond to people's needs... We feel what we are doing is just a drop in the ocean, but that ocean would be less without that drop.

MOTHER TERESA

Why try to get the Light of the Christ from the kingdoms of heaven down to the physical world? So that people can know you are lovely and wonderful and love you and worship you? That's got to be the wrong approach. I would want that Light so I could be of greater service. That service doesn't have time on it, nor any kind of qualifications. It's whatever shows up.

Sometimes we have a hard time getting this Light of the Christ through because of our conditions. Jesus didn't have that problem; His came through so fast, He had a hard time keeping it back in. When He would walk amongst the people they would have spontaneous healing. Even some of the disciples when they walked and the sun shining through their body cast a shadow on a person who was sick, the person got well by the force that came through on the shadow. Now, that's got to be pretty powerful. I mean, how many of you have cast your shadow on people and they've been healed?

Do you understand the power that we're talking about here? That very same power that was with the disciples, if we are to believe what's in the Bible, is with you, too. Jesus said, "I tell you the truth, anyone who has faith in me will do what I have been doing. He will do even greater things than these, because I am going to the Father" [JOHN 14:12].

Now, either He told the truth or He lied. If He lied, don't quote any more scripture, and if He told the truth, you had better get busy and start claiming what He said.

The claiming was made exactly the same way 2000 years ago. It was stated, "Choose you this day whom you will serve... As for me and my house, we will serve the Lord" [JOSHUA 24:15].

Serve, serve, serve. We are to get up and go do it. When we get up out of the chair—Spirit meets us at the point of our action, so we can put one foot in front of the other and serve.

In that serving I think we find the Christ more readily than when we do anything else. How do you know that "ye are my disciples"? That you do love one another. How do we know that you do love one another? Because you help and serve one another. You work with each other, and you support each other.

And the other admonitions are also laid out—such as the one that says don't judge each other.

If we want the Christ, then we choose to forgive rather than to judge.

THE RESTORATION OF THE SPIRIT

Kind words do not cost much though they accomplish much.
They make other people good-natured. They also produce their
own image on men's souls, and a beautiful image it is.

BLAISE PASCAL

What brings us close to each other is when we look at one another and see that we've done a lot of terribly off track things, and we're still okay.

When we look at each other in forgiveness and loving, we partake of the sacrament of communion—spiritually, not physically. And, although there's no bread or wine, we partake of it because the Spirit's present.

We look at our spouse and we see that God the Father, and the Son, and the Holy Spirit is there also, and we enter into that relationship as a covenant to honor the person we're with. Then the healing of Spirit takes place. God's on His throne—meaning the power and the glory has been restored, and being children of that power and glory, we are also restored.

Not only are we restored inside of ourselves, which must happen first, we then are restored to the one that we've been alienated from. This restoration is one of the greatest forms of service that we can do.

The restoration of love, of service, of balance to anyone, is a great, great service. There is none greater.

PART FIVE
Serving and Giving to Love

" There are those who give
   and know not pain in giving,
   nor do they seek joy,
   nor give with mindfulness of virtue;
   They give as in yonder valley
   the myrtle breathes its fragrance into space.
   Through the hands of such as these
   God speaks, and from behind their eyes
   He smiles upon the earth "

KAHLIL GIBRAN

GIVING YOUR LOVE

See first that you yourself deserve to be a giver, and an instrument of giving. For in truth it is life that gives unto life—while you, who deem yourself a giver, are but a witness.

KHALIL GIBRAN

What is the love inside of you unless you give it away? Giving is the manifestation of loving. Without giving, you may be living. But living without loving is only existence, and existence often is a state of lack and an empty hope that someone will come along and save you from all the things that are happening "to" you.

Loving fills the lack and opens the awareness of the inner wisdom and the knowledge that you are the creator of your universe and that nothing happens to you that you do not create, promote, or allow. Loving is that active, dynamic part of you that accepts responsibility for all that you are and will be and lives in a state of open awareness.

The Spirit is eternal and is a gift that will endure forever. Spirit is free, and that means that you can be as free as you are willing to give Spirit away. That willingness to share all of yourself—all that you are—is your freedom.

If you try to grab a hold of Spirit, you defeat yourself; and you lose yourself. Give it away and you will find it returned to you in more ways than you can imagine. You can't fake it. You can't say you are giving and loving and make anyone believe it, unless you demonstrate that giving. It is by your works that you are known, not by your intentions.

People are very perceptive. You can't fool them. Words of love are not necessarily loving. Loving is active. Loving is giving the God that lives within you to the God that lives within all people everywhere. Loving is sharing yourself.

116

Give yourself a gift of loving. Give yourself a gift of completing each day as it comes to a close and of awakening to the newness in you as each new day dawns. As you reside in your loving heart at each and every moment, you find that you reside permanently in the Christ and that you will never be separated from His grace and His presence. And you will experience the living Christ as your Beloved.

THE LOVING TOUCH

Long you'll live and high you'll fly and smiles
you'll give and tears you'll cry and all you touch
and all you see is all your life will ever be.

One of the great ways we can serve is to touch, with love.

I make it a point inside of me that there is always a place inside of me to reach out and touch someone with loving. That's what I work from and in. I know that love is the savior of us all. If a person I am relating to doesn't have enough, the love in me would have enough because it's tied to a greater supply of love. I make no apologies for that to anyone. I don't love because I am after anything. My love is to serve because we love to serve. At the same time, it's a very selfish thing, because I feel the love come back to me. It re-enters into me, and I feel the quality that the person receives.

We want to be touched by the Spirit. We fall in love with the Spirit in a person. That's why we stay together when we're old and haggard, because that Spirit is eternally young and present.

If you withdraw your loving, then you're not in a state of acceptance. If you go into acceptance, you go into serving. If you do cooperation—you're serving. If you're dedicated to a person's well being—you are serving. The observable result of that will be God's energy: enthusiasm. In that state, things don't go neutral. They go into kidding and joking and laughing.

THE SERVER AND THE SERVED

I've met a few people who had to change their jobs in order to change their lives, but I've met many more people who merely had to change their motive toward service in order to change their lives.

PEACE PILGRIM

We need to look at service as not only the one who gives but also the one who receives. For there must be a receiver in order to serve.

God is in the business of service. But in order to be in business, He needs people receiving the service—and that's us.

Looking at service this way, we have to say that both the server and the served are one.

WE SERVE TO LOVE

Give all to love; Obey thy heart.

EMERSON

We serve to love. It's very simple. Because when we serve from the heart, the love will flow through.

We just get in touch with our spiritual self, and we love God and our fellow man, and we serve them and love them so that they know there is love in this world.

One of the primary teachings of Christ is to love your neighbor as yourself. That's difficult because some of you don't have a feeling of high esteem about your capacity to love. Yet no matter how it may seem to you and how it will be looked upon, let your love and Light shine so that the manifestation of God becomes present in everybody—for to withhold yourself is a spiritual crime.

We have God our father and God our mother who sustains our energy in our body, who is us in the body, and we're also the son of that in the body. So we must serve each other as we serve God, because God is in each one of us.

THE SERVICE THAT
TRANSFORMS YOU

Service is nothing but love in work clothes.

JULLAN OF NORWICH

One great key to being aware of your soul is loving the Spirit in your fellow human being. You have then fulfilled two key scriptural admonitions: to love your neighbor as yourself; and when you've done it to the least one of these you've done it unto me.

We certainly get to practice this all the time, day in and day out, with all those petty tyrants who come at us with their criticalness. You don't have to love what they do, but you can love them. What they do can be ignored and forgotten like your last bowel movement or the air that leaves your lungs on an exhale.

All you've got to do is keep loving and serving, because that becomes a spiritual exercise in itself that will transform you.

SERVING SOMEONE UNTIL
THEIR LAST BREATH

We cannot live for ourselves alone. Our lives are connected by a thousand invisible threads, and along these sympathetic fibers, our actions run as causes and return to us as results.

HERMAN MELVILLE

I think you have to be really strong to be a worker in a hospice. I think you need compassion beyond any measure and the passion to go on beyond any fulfillment.

Most people get closest to God at two important points in their lives—at birth and at death.

We come in from God with a message of life, and we return to God with a message of eternal Life. So serving in a hospice is a great way to serve.

It's the time to assist others in making peace with everything in them and around them.

SERVE THE LOVING

Often we can help each other most
by leaving each other alone; at other times
we need the hand-grasp and the word of cheer.

ELBERT HUBBARD

To love God with your body, mind, and soul means being in service to that which is the loving.

It's a simple statement, and we don't have to hold the fear of hell over us in order to get us to do that.

AWAKENING THE INNER VOICE

Kindness is loving people more than they deserve.

JOSEPH JOUBERT

If you don't listen to the inner voice, it shuts off because it's non-inflictive.

To awaken it again takes a lot of prayer, a lot of devotion, a lot of spiritual exercises, and I'll tell you a way it opens in a hurry—be of selfless service to people.

That opens the heart, the spirit heart opens, and the communication of the Lord starts to be with you.

You might want to look at how you can be of greater service, how you can serve in a greater way. If you really served people as though they were the Lord, something magnificent would happen to you, and you would wonder why you didn't do it sooner.

It's when you open inside, to the Lord of your heart, to the Beloved, that you are on a sure path. As you serve unconditionally with loving, you're going to see a lot of us on that path.

THE NATURE OF THE SOUL

How can I be useful, of what service can I be?
There is something inside me, what can it be?

VINCENT VAN GOGH

If I woke up some morning and I wanted to know myself more as a soul. I would access the qualities of soul.

The qualities of soul are loving, caring, and sharing.

The soul is the essence of God. And God loves all of its creation and maintains and serves and gives to it.

I would immediately enter into those attributes—loving, caring, and sharing. I know that I have health, wealth, and happiness because there's prosperity, abundance and riches in all my worlds.

I would walk with that consciousness of loving, caring, and sharing for people. That doesn't mean that you have to wash every toilet in town, but it does mean that someone in need would feel your caring, and that if there is something you can do for them, you would do that.

I would sacrifice a great deal of the attitude of "how about me," and "when do I get mine?" Because I know that is not the nature of the soul.

The nature of the soul is to serve. The Lord said, "To love your neighbor as yourself." To love the soul of your neighbor, you love the soul of yourself. Then you enter into service with your neighbors—which could be laughing and talking with them.

We're here on this planet to work and serve, and to learn and grow. So if we're not doing those things, then we're not doing what we're here to do.

ALWAYS SERVE FROM LOVING

Every day use your magic to be of service to others.

MARCIA WIEDER

Service is something you do willingly from inside of you. Ideally, work should be like that. But often it isn't. Work is often a labor. So we work as a duty.

Your service should always come from loving, caring, and sharing—and also reaching out and touching. Touching opens the spirit of the other person. Sometimes our work won't allow us to reach out in that way.

If we are loving and we are caring, then our touch will convey that. It's comforting, nurturing.

When we can find the work that can be our service, we feel that God is in Heaven. We look forward to it. There aren't many jobs like that, but we can have that experience inside when we approach our life as one of service.

We cannot control the world, but we can control how we act within ourselves, in the world. That's where we have authority, and we can develop the talent to do just that.

The world gives you every opportunity to grow. Opportunity knocks and knocks and knocks and knocks until you answer. Sometimes it hits you in the head! It's just trying to get your attention. So if you're sensitive when it just knocks a little, you'll say, "Okay, I'll serve." You can do it lovingly and joyfully because you have that choice inside.

Service is what you do that you do freely, without expectation of return.

CUT YOURSELF SOME SLACK

Service to a just cause rewards the worker
with more real happiness and satisfaction
than any other venture of life.

CARRIE CHAPMAN CATT

No one ever moves directly towards the sun all the time. It can't be done.

You have to sometimes get out of the heat and stop being so "spiritual" and ground yourself a bit.

I've made it a point to never sit in judgment of people's actions. Because if somebody's sitting down having a beer or two, you may not know that they've been out serving four thousand people, ministering night and day, and they're taking a rest. So you just let everything go like it is.

Sometimes we need to back off from things because it gets intense. So, let's cut each other a whole lot of slack. And cut yourself a lot, too, while you are at it.

Do you know what cutting a lot of slack means? Don't be tied so close to things. Cut yourself loose, cut your mind loose and your emotions loose once in a while; you know, say, "Gosh, darn it!" once in a while just to keep in contact with the rest of the world who says that.

RAISING YOUR VIBRATION LEVEL

It is not the style of clothes one wears, neither the kind of automobile one drives, nor the amount of money one has in the bank, that counts. These mean nothing. It is simply service that measures success.

GEORGE WASHINGTON CARVER

Being of service is the best way to deal with the self-obsession that is so prevalent in this world.

Being of service just for the joy of doing it will raise your vibration level, and you will rise above the voices of self-doubt, second-guessing, and negativity.

The lower vibration voices cannot survive. They will not live in that atmosphere of joy and serving because they think of, "Me first, me only. And forget you."

So it's quite easy to transcend these lower levels when we move into service.

THE NEXT MASS EXODUS TO VENUS

Love your life, perfect your life, beautify all things in your life. Seek to make your life long and of service to your people. When you rise in the morning, give thanks for the light, for your life, for your strength. Give thanks for your food and for the joy of living. If you see no reason to give thanks, the fault lies in yourself.

TECUMSEH

Service is the highest form of consciousness on this planet. You've probably read that several times in this book.

I've hesitated to go into all this detail about serving before, because a lot of people then get caught up in the details and the words and never get out there and actually serve.

My bottom line: Whatever it is, no matter how minute your service is, do it.

Some people are waiting for a great big opportunity to serve. As if they're waiting to take hundreds of people on the next mass exodus to Venus. Well, if you are one of those people, the spaceship left four thousand years ago. They're gone. You are out of a job. You're waiting to make a big impact where you will be recognized and idolized. Can you see how the negative-voice syndrome asserts itself?

So start serving in small ways now. Yes, by all means, work every day to better yourself. Indeed, affirm, "Every day, in every way, I'm getting better and better," but that by itself is not sufficient. You've got to go to the interior of yourself, into your humanness, into the loving, caring, serving place inside of you. By going in there, you will already have served yourself, taken care of yourself, and loved yourself; because when you're in that place, it is loving. It is affection. It is the Spirit.

129

When you are filled with that, it flows out of you into the world. People will say, "I just feel this loving coming out of you; what are you doing?" You'll say, "I haven't done anything. I just walked in the room. I want to follow the Spirit of truth. So I spend time within. That's how I am of service to myself."

THANK GOD WE CAN SERVE

You've no doubt heard that we live in a service economy, but have you thought about the implications of that term?

To be of service means to be helpful.

To pursue a successful career or to build a prosperous business in a service economy, you have to be helpful. The more helpful you are and the more people you are helpful to, the more successful and prosperous you are likely to be yourself.

JOE TYE

This world is being run, through us, by the God power. And we can conduct this power out here into the world through our loving service.

It's very ordinary—to do the work wherein nobody knows who did it. The consciousness of God that resides in you, and who is you, notes it and uses that serving consciousness to build up inside of you the ability to do even more.

Thank God that we can serve the Light that God has put here in us. Thank God that we can serve the Sound of God here in us.

Many of us know that we are coming to a crossroads on the planet, and we need to choose which way we're going to go with our life—whether we're going to continue on living it for our own personal gain or whether we're going to live it for the gain of humanity.

There have been a few themes that keep coming up throughout this book—loving your neighbor as yourself, being of unconditional service, and living a life of personal integrity.

If you have taken another position, get off it and move to the spirit of service. Which means make sure you're loving yourself in such a way that the neighbor will get that you love them. When you've done that, you've really been of service.

UNCONDITIONAL LOVING

*Those who are lifting the world upward and onward
are those who encourage more than criticize.*

ELIZABETH HARRISON

Unconditional loving is loving unconditionally. In that unconditional place, there is not a thought of getting anything in return. It is service of the highest nature to just love, because that is your nature. And even more than that, to go ahead and put your mind and your emotions and your body on it and move out there in the world of illusion, deceit, intrigue, and all the dilemma of life, and stand there as an unconditional lover, loving unconditionally, regardless.

When it rains and there's thunder and lightning, and the people strike at you, know that they do so because they hurt and they have lost track of their own unconditional loving of themselves. The job to be done is for you to once again start loving yourself in their presence, not tell them, "You forgot to love yourself." They don't want to hear that. They want to know, "How do I love myself?" And it's very simple. Think happy thoughts. Feel happy thoughts. Have happy feet and get busy just having a hell of a good time.

If you're afraid of making a fool out of yourself, then to hell with you, because that's where you're going to go inside of you anyway. Who cares what people think? Have fun all the time just doing nutty, crazy things called loving people and loving yourself. And have happy hands, too, and get to feel happy and enthusiastic inside. Don't even care what you think, because thinking is not infinity and who you are is infinite.

A long time ago, I said that God is in control here, and whatever the game God has going for all of us, we participate because there is no real choice. We can choose to participate out of negativity, out of doubt, out of superstition, out of a lot of things, and it's okay because you're the one in there with all of that, choosing to play the game that way.

You could also choose to participate out of the joy of serving and giving, and come into a higher state of life on this planet. No one is exempt from anything here. But who cares for an exemption when you're inheriting the Kingdom? The good news is that, after everyone's in the Kingdom, there will be nobody left to hold the depressions, the negativity in the world.

SACRIFICING ANGER

The contents of Sitting Bull's pockets were often emptied into the hands of small, ragged little boys, nor could he understand how so much wealth should go brushing by, unmindful of the poor.

ANNIE OAKLEY

If you are feeling angry, I would sacrifice the anger on the altar of love.

Transmute the energy from anger to love.

I wouldn't get rid of the anger energy—just change it into love energy. So as much anger as you had before, you've now got that much more love to share.

But I'd get a dose of that love for myself first.

I'd make sure that all the cells of my body are feeling that loving and that caring and that nurturing because I'm living in there, and I want that body to serve as the temple of the Spirit in the best way possible.

WHAT BUILDS YOUR CHARACTER

We will receive not what we idly wish for but
what we justly earn. Our rewards will always
be in exact proportion to our service.

EARL NIGHTINGALE

In the Spirit there is no one really higher than the other. One of the most important commandments is to "love one another," and that loving one another wasn't based upon any condition. It was simply a statement of "Love one another."

At the last supper, Jesus washed everyone's feet, showing that to serve one another is to love one another and that we're dealing with a spiritual consciousness of opening up and giving forth to the people around you.

Serving is what really builds your character. It's what ethics are based upon. It's what your morality will be based upon.

A SACRED AND HOLY ACTION

There is no more noble occupation in the world than to assist another human being—to help someone succeed.

ALAN LOY MCGINNIS

There may be a whole lot of places you'll walk through in this world, and you're going to think, "What am I doing here?" because you're not getting anything out of being there.

Perhaps you can shift your attitude at that point and say, "I am here to give."

Be giving of the peace and the quiet of your being into that particular place so that someone who comes along may undergo a change in consciousness. If they are down, they may draw upon the peace you placed there, and lift, and be free.

That can really be a terrific service. That silent action, to me, gets to be real sacred and holy and special.

ENOUGH LOVE BUT
NOT ENOUGH LOVING

The ultimate all of us have to learn is unconditional love,
which includes not only others but ourselves as well.

ELISABETH KUBLER-ROSS

Loving, caring, and sharing—those words are spelled with "i-n-g," on the end. It isn't love, care, and share. It's loving, caring, and sharing.

Somebody once said that enough love will save the planet. I told them that there's enough love on this planet, but there's not enough loving. That loving can be as simple as scratching your spouse's back when it itches, or helping people out when they need a ride.

The key is to put your body out there in service. And don't judge the action, which is the caring for yourself and the others. The sharing is what naturally takes place.

I came to the conclusion for me that the highest form of consciousness we can manifest physically is service to humanity. That service has got to come from the place inside of willingness in the serving.

It doesn't have to have anything worthwhile to serve, it just has to serve willingly, openly, lovingly, caringly. There are benefits that appear after you've done that called health, wealth, and happiness.

I think happiness is something that just appears inside of you, where you're content with you and with the Lord.

Call it a principle, a unity, call it one mind, one God, one consciousness, one voice—call it any of that. It doesn't matter to me what you call it. I just call it "Beloved."

SPIRITUAL EXERCISES, UNCONDITIONAL LOVING, AND SERVICE

Doing service is a powerful way to open the heart and fulfill the soul. Those people who do service know how much joy they receive from giving to others.

MARGARET PAUL

It takes a great amount of energy to resist upset or negativity, to push it away, that's why we feel it deeply inside of us as a total commitment. In this way, we get committed more towards negativity, because we have put more energy towards it than we ever put towards the positive. It's why negative things affect us more dramatically than positive things. Just look at your life!

Through the years, I have said three things consistently, "Do spiritual exercises. Be as unconditionally loving as you can. And be of service."

Are you volunteering your time to organizations that are structured towards upliftment and to the unity of Spirit in mankind—as a loving, caring approach to existence?

If you say that your work is that, I say that it is what you are being paid for. The service that I am talking about is receiving no payment, like breathing in. I don't get a reward for that because the breath is the reward. As soon as I breathe my reward is instantaneous. I'm alive. Being of unconditional service does the same thing.

You don't serve for acknowledgement or respect. You serve for that immediate payment of serving. That is extremely important. Coupled with spiritual exercises, being of service is one of the greatest forms of demonstrating the inner consciousness of loving out here in the world. It has nothing to do with serving as a do-gooder. In its higher form, it is more the anonymous type of service where nobody really knows that you did do it.

My ministry is a secret ministry. For the most part, what I really do is never seen. So there's really no way you can say thanks to me. It's kept hidden away. It's not "secret" that I can't tell it; it's secret in terms of sacred.

A man, at Christmas time, gave away some $10,000 in $100 bills to various people. People were asking him who he was. He answered that if he told them, it would ruin what he was doing. The giving of it was his immediate reward—a silent service to many people. His being anonymous was maintained, and the sacredness of his gift was integrated into himself and the other person.

Dry spells in spiritual exercises are often the signal for wet spells of service. Go out there and water God's flowers. I'm not saying to go and give money—maybe you don't have the money—but certainly give of yourself.

THE BELOVED'S UNCONDITIONAL SERVICE

Love expects no reward. Love knows no fear. Love Divine gives —does not demand. Love thinks no evil; imputes no motive. To Love is to share and serve.

SIVANANDA

Do you sense the presence of the Beloved? It can be done through feeling or seeing or hearing or touching or smelling or tasting.

Even if you don't make yourself available to it, it is always available to you.

The Beloved is always available to us because it doesn't respect our thoughts or our feelings about it. If we say it's not here, it doesn't pay any attention to that statement. It still stays present and readily available, because it's of unconditional service.

LIVING THE LIFE OF A SAINT

One man can completely change the character
of a country, and the industry of its people,
by dropping a single seed in fertile soil.

JOHN C. GIFFORD

When our thoughts bring us towards service and oneness, we know those thoughts are of God, because God is One. There is no second.

If your thoughts take you away from the loving of your spouse, your children, or your neighbor, you just should know that you are dwelling in darkness.

It's when your thoughts bring you to unity and upliftment, service, and the oneness, and support and the caring; it's then that you are living the life of a saint, for you are doing what they did.

When you see people open their heart, that's all the thanks you really need.

SERVING TO CLEAR KARMA

In about the same degree as you are helpful,
you will be happy.

KARL REILAND

The kindness of the Spirit protects us from seeing what terrible things we have done in past existences so we don't sit around and spend the rest of this lifetime crying about the awful thing we did in the twelfth century to all the people we were with back then.

Doing your spiritual exercises (s.e.'s) and being of service are the best ways I know to balance the karma of the past. That's why we say to do s.e.'s and be of service. And often we say, be of service and do s.e.'s because that's really more important for the person. However, being of service is not a substitute for spiritual exercises.

The service we speak about is not the service for recognition. It's a service of silence. You just go and do things for people. Perhaps it's being a guardian angel for someone. If it's someone that you like a lot, it may not count too much. But if it's somebody you detest, good— that may count greatly in your favor.

Usually, when you have done service to somebody you detest, you start to find out things about them that are very wonderful. Then you're taken away from service to them to serve somebody else that you detest, but you find out that you can start to love people because there is a lovableness in all of them.

LAYING UP THE TREASURES IN HEAVEN

How far that little candle throws his beams!
So shines a good deed in a naughty world.

SHAKESPEARE

Being of service is not trying to fathom the depth of some other being in order to find yourself, because you will only find that you've wasted your time with somebody who's going to be gone and whom you may never see again in any existence.

But if you fathom the depth of yourself and you find your own true being, then you'll be with all the other beings that have found themselves. Then you are living with the saints, also called living in the kingdom of God.

There's a lot of ways to attain this. If you just pray, that won't be enough. But if you pray and then you look to be of service, that's going to fulfill a big part of the process. In reaching out a helping hand to others, you're going to find within you the answers that really matter.

And many people, when you go to help them, are going to say, "Please don't." Believe it or not, leaving them alone is also laying up the treasures in heaven, because instead of doing good we can easily start to impose ourselves and become do-gooders. The result is that we often end up doing bad.

Our service is really quite simple then, isn't it? Love God with all your body, mind, and soul and your neighbor as yourself, and when you've done it to the least one of these, you've done it unto me. Wow.

We say it in this current time as "take care of yourself so you can help take care of others; don't hurt yourself and don't hurt others; and use everything for your upliftment, learning and growth." Those actions lay up the treasures in the kingdom of heaven. All we did was modernize the language.

PART SIX

Tools for Givers

We discussed earlier the concept of
sending the Light for the highest good.
This is a fundamental tool.

Enclosed in this section are a few others.

> " Do all the good you can,
>   By all the means you can,
>   In all the ways you can,
>   In all the places you can,
>   At all the times you can,
>   To all the people you can,
>   As long as ever you can. "

JOHN WESLEY

ACCEPTANCE

This is the true joy in life, the being used for a purpose recognized by yourself as a mighty one; the being thoroughly worn out before you are thrown on the scrap heap; the being a force of nature instead of a feverish selfish little clod of ailments and grievances complaining that the world will not devote itself to making you happy.

GEORGE BERNARD SHAW

Acceptance is such an important commodity; it's the first law of Spirit. In the context of this book, we could also call it the first law of giving.

Acceptance is simply seeing something the way it is and saying, "That's the way it is."

Acceptance is not approval, consent, permission, authorization, sanction, concurrence, agreement, compliance, sympathy, endorsement, confirmation, support, ratification, assistance, advocating, backing, maintaining, authenticating, reinforcing, cultivating, encouraging, furthering, promoting, aiding, abetting, or even *liking* what is.

Acceptance is saying, "It is what it is, and what is, is what is." Until we truly accept *everything*, we can never see clearly and seldom give appropriately. We will always be looking through the filters of "must's," "should's," "ought-to's," "have-to's", and prejudices.

When reality confronts our notion of what reality *should* be, reality always wins. (Drop something while believing gravity *shouldn't* make it fall. It falls anyway.) Usually we don't like this (that is, we have trouble *accepting* this), so we either struggle with reality and become upset, or turn away from it and become unconscious. If you find yourself upset or unconscious about something, or alternating

147

between the two, you might ask yourself, "What am I not accepting about this?"

Acceptance is not a state of passivity or inaction. We are obviously not saying you can't change the world, right wrongs, or replace evil with good. Acceptance is the first step to successful service.

If you don't fully accept a situation precisely the way it is, you may get caught up trying to change it. Moreover, if you don't fully accept the situation, you will never really know if the situation *can* be changed.

LET GO, RELAX

The noblest service comes from nameless hands,
And the best servant does his work unseen.

OLIVER WENDELL HOLMES

When you accept, you relax; you let go; you become patient. This is an enjoyable (and effective) place for either participation or departure. To stay and struggle (even for fun things: how many times have you tried *really hard* to have a good time?) or to run away in disgust or fear are not the most fulfilling ways to live or give. It is, however, the inevitable result of non-acceptance.

Take a few moments and consider a situation you are not happy with—not your greatest burden in life, just a simple event about which you feel peeved. Now accept *everything* about the situation. Let it be the way it is. Because, after all, it is that way, is it not? Also, if you accept it, you will feel better about it.

After accepting it, and everything about it, you probably still won't *like* it, but you may stop disliking or fearing it. At worst, you will hate it or fear it a little less.

That's the true value of acceptance: you feel better about life and about yourself. Everything I've said about acceptance applies to things you have done (or failed to do) as well. In fact, everything I've said about acceptance applies *especially* to areas in your life where you judge yourself.

All the things you think you should have done that you didn't do, and all the things you did that you think you shouldn't have done, accept them. You did (or didn't) do them. That's reality. That's what happened. There's no changing the past. You can struggle with the past or pretend it didn't happen, or you can accept it. We suggest the latter. A life of guilt, fear, and unconsciousness is, to say the least, not much fun. It also takes a lot of time and energy away from giving.

ACCEPTING THE FUTURE

Blessed is he who expects no gratitude,
for he shall not be disappointed.

W. C. BENNETT

While you're at it, you might as well accept all your future transgressions against the "should's," "must's," and "have-to's" of this world. You will transgress. Not that we necessarily *endorse* transgression. We do, however, accept the fact that human beings do such things; and if you haven't yet accepted your humanity, with all the magnificence and folly inherent in that, now might be a good time to start.

Relax. Accept what's already taken place whether done by you or someone or something outside of you. Then look for the gift you are able to give and the best way of giving it. Acceptance lays the foundation for service. Forgiveness wipes the slate clean so you can serve freely.

FOR GIVING

Forgiveness is the giving, and so the receiving, of life.

GEORGE MACDONALD

Forgiving means "for giving"—*for*, in favor of; *giving*, to give. When you forgive another, to whom do you give? The other? Sometimes. Yourself? Always. To forgive another is being *in favor of giving* to yourself and to others.

In addition, most of us judge ourselves more harshly and more often than we judge others. It's important to forgive ourselves for all the things we hold against ourselves.

There is a third thing to forgive: the fact that we ever judged in the first place. When we judge, we leave our happiness behind—sometimes way behind. We know this, and we judge ourselves for having judged in the first place.

There are two layers of forgiveness: first, the person we judged (ourselves or another); and, second, ourselves for having judged in the first place.

The technique? Simple. So simple, that some people doubt its effectiveness and don't try it. We urge you to try it.

Say to yourself, "I forgive   (name of the person, situation, or thing you judged, including yourself) for (the "transgression"). I forgive myself for judging (same person, situation, or thing, including yourself) for (what you judged)."

That's it. Simple but amazingly effective. You can say it out loud or say it to yourself. But, please, do say it.

That's all there is to forgiveness. Simple but powerful. How powerful? Do five minutes of forgiveness. See what happens.

FOR GETTING

If you have much Give of your wealth,
If you have little Give of your heart.

SHAKESPEARE

After you've forgiven the transgression and the judgment, there's only one thing to do: forget them. Whatever "protection" you think you may gain from remembering all your past grievances is far less important than the balm of forgetting.

What's the value in forgetting? It's all in the word: for getting—to be in favor of getting, of receiving.

If you have a clenched fist, it is difficult to receive. If you let go and open the fist, you have a hand. Then it's easy to receive. And to give.

We sometimes think that shaking a fist (threateningly, with all the remembered transgressions) is the way to get something. A shaking fist tends to beget a shaking (or swinging) fist.

To receive, for give. To get, for get. To give, for give and for get.

The space in your consciousness (mind, body, emotions) that's remembering a grievance is locked into remembering hurt, pain, anger, betrayal, and disappointment. Who on earth wants to remember that? Let it go. For give it away. Then for *get* something new, better, and lighter in its place. Then you have something more valuable inside you from which to give.

153

Heal the memories. Forgive the past. Then forget it. **Let it go**. It is not worth remembering. None of it is worth remembering. What's worth *experiencing* and *giving* is the joy of this moment. Sound good?

SERVING FREE OF KARMA

Many of the greatest things man has achieved are not the result of consciously directed thought, and still less the product of a deliberately coordinated effort of many individuals, but of a process in which the individual plays a part which he can never fully understand.

FREDRICH AUGUST VON HAYEK

The key to serving, and in fact the key to anything you do, is your attitude.

If you are of genuine service—not your idea of service but the compatibility that what you are serving is needed and wanting to be received—then the action is probably going to be free of karma.

If you feel really good about what you did, you probably picked up something, like an ego trip.

If you walk away saying, "Well, I don't know what happened there, maybe it was good, maybe it wasn't, I don't know," you probably did well, because there's no ego trip.

If there's no karma, there's no playback, no information. You wouldn't know anything one way or another. You honestly say, "I don't know." And that can be a really good place to be.

SACRIFICE

Life is made up, not of great sacrifices or duties, but of little things, in which smiles and kindness, and small obligations given habitually, are what preserve the heart and secure comfort.

WILLIAM DAVY

You would be far happier if you gave up certain things. This may not be easy for you. We nonetheless suggest you give them up—go cold turkey—starting right now, this minute, before you turn the page.

Give is an up word. *Up* is an up word. Put them together, and people get awfully down. "I'm not going to give up *anything.* And *sacrifice.* That's even *worse* than giving up. Sacrifice means giving up something *really* good."

The things we think you'd be better off sacrificing are things such as greed, lust, hurt, judgments, demands, spoiledness, envy, jealousy, and vindictiveness.

Did you think we were going to ask you to give up good stuff? Most people think that sacrifice means giving up only the good stuff. Not so. The negative stuff, the cold stuff, the hard stuff—you can sacrifice those, too.

And you can give them up. Surrender them to the higher part of yourself. Surround them with Light. Let them go.

You don't need them anymore.

Giving these things up will give immeasurable gifts to you and all those you come into contact with.

THE EXAMPLE OF ST. FRANCIS

Serve wholeheartedly as if you were serving the Lord, not men. Because you know the Lord will reward everyone for whatever good he does, whether he is slave or free.

EPHESIANS 6:5

The nice thing about St. Francis of Assisi is that he saw the Lord in so many ways and in so many forms. It's very easy to see God when things are wonderful and very beautiful and warm and there's great fellowship. But it takes far greater courage to see that same face of God when it's cold, when there's no food, when there's been trouble with your spouse, when there's care and worry about people dying, when there's hunger in the world.

We have an example in our brother Francis and our sister Clare, who a long time ago, in a time that was even more difficult than now, put their bodies on the line. They didn't put out words or opinions. They sought out the Lord in that sacred place inside that we know, asking "Lord, what do you want me to do?" In that the Lord often showed them the next step, and I'd be willing to bet that the Lord even pushed them a few steps.

One thing that seemed to be very prevalent in St. Francis' work was one of the greatest commandments—that you do love one another. All of you reading this book are loving, caring people; otherwise, you would not be attracted to a book on service. But often those qualities slip away. Often that glamour of the world, the distraction of the personality, takes you far away from where the Lord lives inside of you and that kingdom wherein we are the heirs, where we will get to live with Brother Francis, Sister Clare, all the other saints known and unknown, and to live with the Christ, the living Lord. Therefore, we have a very wonderful task in front of us, and that task is to place in us the remembrance of these moments of communion, where the most sacred communion takes place. Where we tell God, we tell the Lord, the saints, we tell our parents who have passed over, that in us we have a sanctuary for the most high, for the most wonderful things and that we will constantly cleanse it. We will cleanse all the children of darkness from it— the habits of our personality that no longer serve us. We'll cleanse the excess of materiality from us, so that we only have that which we can use. That use is to be of service to other people. And if it can't serve others, then the use must be passed on. It frees us then from those attachments to this world that would block us from eating and drinking of the love and the Light, and especially of the Sound—that unspoken word of God.

St. Francis is alive in our hearts, and our Spirit, and when we hear the song, *"Brother Sun, Sister Moon,"* it does not exclude anyone. It includes everything in this world, for it's all the handwork of the Lord. Keep this one a remembrance, that you come to it daily for even a second. That you refresh yourself. That you gain the strength to love yourself, to love others. Mother Theresa once said to me, "You did it unto me." It's important to remember that.

Put the Light of God high in your ideals—not so high that you can confuse it or dilute it. But high enough that when you need to make decisions in this world, you can reach into that ideal Light and look on this world with the compassion that it needs. And there, ask the Lord, "What do you want me to do for You?" That "for You" means for all of the people. And then listen to the Lord's answer. He may speak to you, you may feel Him, you may sense it, or you may find yourself arising from your moment of prayer and moving on something new that is inspired out of you by this essence of love that we know is God.

158

SEEDING AND TITHING

Tithing and seeding, done with the right attitude of giving, can open your Spirit and bring you to an inner peace inside, by balancing some of the karmic blocks that have stood in your way.

And if, on top of that, you get the material things, you're getting your cake and eating it too.

Tithing is about placing God first in your life. Being a joyful giver is a great part of loving the Lord with your body, mind, and Soul.

Seeding and tithing are two important aspects of giving. One is saying "please"; the other is saying "thank you."

Seeding is planting the crop. Tithing is saying "thank you" when the harvest is in. Tithing and Seeding are a physical affirmation of both abundance and gratitude.

It's very hard for people to shake you loose from your Spirit if you're doing both tithing and seeding.

Seeding and tithing are acknowledging the *source* of our good, our abundance. The source can be represented by whatever we choose—whichever organization or person represents the highest good we know. The acknowledgement is in the form of *money*.

Money? Yes, money. Giving away *money* shows we really *mean it*. Just *whom* does it show we really mean it? Why, *ourselves*, of course. And it shows the comfort zone too. There's little the comfort zone has a tighter hold on than the purse strings. If you can give away *money*—in set amounts and at regular intervals—your mastery of the comfort zone is well under way, and your giving moves into high gear.

Seeding is giving money away before you achieve something. As its name implies, it is planting a seed. What would it be worth to you—in terms of hard cash—to have your service in a specific area be successful? Seed from one to ten percent of that amount. How do you seed? Send a check to the organization or person that represents—in your estimation—the highest power for good, and let it go.

Don't tell *anyone* that you have seeded for something until *after* you have achieved it.

Tithing is giving away ten percent of your material increase. If you make $1,000, give $100 of it away. If someone gives you something worth $1,000, give $100 (in cash or valuable asset) away.

Why? By tithing, you make a statement of abundance to yourself. You are saying, "Thank you. I have more than I need." To consistently give away ten percent of your increase indicates—through action—that you are a conscientious user of energy. Those who waste energy, it seems, are given less and less. Those who make good use of it are given more and more. Tithing demonstrates you are a good manager of resources.

Seeding and tithing in set amounts on a regular basis keeps your abundance flowing. From that abundance and that overflow, you can give even more than the amount you seed and tithe. In order to give, however, you must have a flow of abundance, and we have found this flow of abundance is best obtained by seeding and tithing.

Where do you give your money? To the source of your spiritual teachings. If you have no spiritual or religious affiliation (the traditional depository of seeding and tithing), you can give to your favorite charity or social cause.

Just so it represents to you the *highest* and *best* work being done in the world, any organization—or person—is fine.

One more thought: if you give begrudgingly, it will be given unto you begrudgingly. If you give joyfully, it will be given unto you joyfully.

Don't wait to give, however, until you can do it joyfully. Start small by tithing 1/2 percent. At least get in the game!

SERVING IN HOSPITALS

Treat people as if they were what they ought to be and
you help them to become what they are capable of being.

GOETHE

Love yourself first, then love your neighbor as yourself. So the loving begins inside of you. Fill yourself with it and then let the overflow go to the neighbor. That way you'll always be able to serve. It's not a ritual. It's an energy field. And we often have to present our bodies there as a conductor of the energy.

Just being physically present is often enough. What's going to happen is already taking place. When you serve in a hospital, you may become aware of negative energies that are there. There's a lot of healing energy, but there is also a lot of ectoplasmic energy (see glossary) in hospitals that negatively affects people without them being conscious of it.

Your being there, using the Light for the highest good, will start to diffuse negativity. Maybe one visit does it and maybe a hundred does it.

Hospitals can be very negative. They're supposed to be temples of healing, but often they can be a pit stop on the way to the grave. There's a lot of death and fear energy there, and a lot of people get sick going to the hospital. In fact, with all that goes with being in a hospital, it turns out to be one of the leading causes of death in the United States.

Health authorities are trying to clean it up, but they don't realize that a lot of the disease comes in on an energy field. The good news is that it also can leave on an energy field.

It is not unlikely that, after you've served in a hospital, you'll walk out with a lot of this type of energy around you.

When you are done, bathe or shower as soon as possible. Also, if you can, change into different clothes when you leave. Dress in clothes just for serving in a hospital and have them cleaned regularly.

Note: Also see "clearing technique" in glossary.

WE ARE HERE TO SERVE
EACH OTHER

God gives skill, but not without men's hands:
He could not make Antonio Stradivari's violins
without Antonio.

ANTONIO STRADIVARI

Everyone must be willing to sacrifice. Do you know what sacrifice means? The first part of the word "sacrifice" means holy. From that perspective, sacrifice no longer goes into suffering.

Sacrifice goes into holiness, into peace, into calmness, and the real willingness to give to others. We will actually sacrifice our time and give it to others. That's service.

We are here to serve each other.

When we get married, we often just serve that one other person; but let's do that fully and in a consciousness of loving. The same principle applies when we raise and serve a family. Get your priorities lined up in the correct order. The highest order of priorities is the human life.

We have to trust that it is going to work out right. We don't close our eyes; we don't go stupid and say, "I'll leave it to the Light." We are the Light. We keep watching, and when we see it not working, we do something. So we have to reach into a place inside that goes past the feeling of "I can't serve." I don't know what it is you feel you can't do, because there is always something that anyone can do.

A PRAYER TO BE OF SERVICE

Let's pray together:

> " *Lord God of creation, again we're here, humbly waiting. Always open, praying, seeking, waiting for Your reply, looking for the next step, wanting to have that direction of service that is Yours.*
>
> *In this do I find my greatest happiness and joy.*
>
> *In this do I find my greatest calling of the heart.*
>
> *In this do I willingly sacrifice the world.*
>
> *For in this, I gain myself, for it's not of the world.*
>
> *It's of You. And it's You I seek, over and over. And one day I shall surely find you, and we shall find that that oneness has always been the Beloved.*
>
> *I only pray to make myself available to You, as I know you've always been available to me.*
>
> *Keep the heart open and the eyes firm, and the mind steady on this that I have chosen to come into You.*
>
> *Let that that would distract me be placed away for others who need to learn of that. But keep me in the heart of Your heart. And keep me in the hearts of my fellow men, that in that place where I reside with them, they find comfort, and that I am not a stumbling block for them. That they would look upon me with a joy, and with the pleasure of saying: "He's my friend." This, then, is the way the cosmic force of love and Light works.*
>
> *Amen, Lord.* "

If you care to have that as your own, you may just silently say Amen.

If you don't like the level you're on,
move to a higher one.

The higher one can be reached
through meditation,
through spiritual exercises.
And it can be reached most definitely through service.

JOHN-ROGER

GLOSSARY

BELOVED: *The soul; the God within.*

CLEARING TECHNIQUE: *The first thing is to ask for the Light and the Traveler to help you release anything that is not for your highest good. Also, here is a general clearing technique you can use to clear people, places, things, etc., from yourself: you put the palm of one hand over your forehead and say the name of the person (or whatever; we can call it X) and then say, "Anything from or through X, clear, disengage, disconnect." (You can also say something like "cut off," or any other verb that gets across, to you, what you would like to take place.) Then, while your hand is still on your forehead, you ask that this be done through the Traveler, Christ, and Holy Spirit, for the highest good of all concerned—and you have the intention that it will clear completely.*

ECTOPLASMIC ENERGY: *A field of energy that can build up over time and permeate a physical environment—walls, furniture, carpets, drapes, etc. It can be positive or negative and may be related to events and experiences that have taken place in that environment over time.*

LIGHT: *The energy of Spirit that pervades all realms of existence. Also refers to the Light of the Holy Spirit.*

LIGHT COLUMNS. *One can ask for, and visualize, a column of pure Light extending from the heavens, through them and into the core of the earth. Let's just say also that we should all be Light columns first. Physically, mentally, emotionally, spiritually, we should be a Light column. Then, wherever we go, wherever we sit, wherever we talk, we should leave a column of our beingness of Light there.*

SOUND OF GOD, OR SOUND CURRENT: *The audible energy that flows from God through all realms. The spiritual energy on which a person returns to the heart of God.*

SPIRITUAL EXERCISES (S.E.'S): *An active technique of bypassing the mind and emotions by using a spiritual tone to connect to the Sound Current. Assists a person in breaking through the illusions of the lower levels and eventually moving into Soul consciousness*

TRAVELER, OR MYSTICAL TRAVELER: *The Mystical Traveler is a spiritual consciousness that exists throughout all levels of God's creation. It resides within each person and is a guide into the higher levels of Spirit, the greater reality of God.*

ADDITIONAL RESOURCES & STUDY MATERIALS BY JOHN-ROGER, D.S.S.

The following books and audio materials can support you in learning more about the ideas presented in Serving & Giving. *They can be ordered through the Movement of Spiritual Inner Awareness at:* **1-800-899-2665**, *order@msia.org, or simply visit our online store at www.msia.org*

FORGIVENESS: THE KEY TO THE KINGDOM

Forgiveness is the key factor in personal liberation and spiritual progression. This book presents profound insights into forgiveness and the resulting personal joy and freedom. God's business is forgiving. This book provides encouragement and techniques for making it our business as well.

Softbound Book #0914829629, **$12.95**

MOMENTUM: LETTING LOVE LEAD— SIMPLE PRACTICES FOR SPIRITUAL LIVING

(with Paul Kaye, D.S.S.)

As much as we might like to have the important areas of our lives—Relationships, Health, Finances and Career—all settled and humming along, the reality for most of us is that there is always something out of balance, often causing stress and distress. Rather than resisting or regretting imbalance, this book shows that there is an inherent wisdom in imbalance. Where there is imbalance, there is movement, and that movement "gives rise to a dynamic, engaging life that is full of learning, creativity, and growth."

We can discover—in the very areas where we experience most of our problems and challenges—the greatest movement and the greatest opportunity for change.

The approach is not to try harder at making life work. Life already works. The big key is to bring loving into it. This book is about being loving in the moment. It is a course in loving.

Hardbound book #1893020185, **$19.95**

THE REST OF YOUR LIFE *(with Paul Kaye, D.S.S.)*
What if you discovered that rest is less an action and more an attitude? That you can gain all the inner and outer benefits of rest as you move through each day, no matter how busy you are? Here is the good news: It's true, and you can. If you ever told yourself you could do with a good rest, this book will serve you well. Starting now, for the rest of your life.

Softbound book # 9781893020436, **$16.95**

WHEN ARE YOU COMING HOME? A PERSONAL GUIDE TO SOUL TRANSCENDENCE *(with Pauli Sanderson, D.S.S.)*
An intimate account of spiritual awakening that contains the elements of an adventure story. How did John-Roger attain the awareness of who he truly is? He approached life like a scientist in a laboratory. He found methods for integrating the sacred with the mundane, the practical with the mystical. He noted what worked and what didn't. Along with some fascinating stories, you will find in this book many practical keys for making your own life work better, for attuning to the source of wisdom that is always within you, and for making every day propel you further on your exciting adventure home.

Hardbound book # 1893020231, **$19.95**

WHAT'S IT LIKE BEING YOU? *(with Paul Kaye, D.S.S.)*
"What would happen if you stopped doing what you thought you were supposed to be doing and started being who you are?" The sequel to their previous book together, Momentum – Letting Love Lead, *this book features exercises, meditations and narrative to deepen and explore who you really are as well as a new CD release "Meditation for Alignment with the True Self".*

Softbound book #:1893020258, **$14.95**

SPIRITUAL WARRIOR: THE ART OF SPIRITUAL LIVING
Full of wisdom, humor, common sense, and hands-on tools for spiritual living, this book offers practical tips to take charge of our lives and create greater health, happiness, abundance, and loving. Becoming a spiritual warrior has nothing to do with violence. It is about using the positive qualities of the spiritual warrior—intention, ruthlessness, and impeccability—to counter negative personal habits and destructive relationships, especially when you are confronted with great adversity.

Softbound book #9781893020481, **$14.95**

THE TAO OF SPIRIT

This beautifully designed collection of writings is intended to free you from outer worldly distractions and guide your return to the stillness within. The Tao of Spirit *can provide daily inspirations and new approaches on how to handle stress and frustration. What a wonderful way to start or to end the day—remembering to let go of your day-to-day problems and be refreshed in the source at the center of your existence. Many people use this book in preparation for meditation or prayer.*

Hardbound book #0914829335, **$15**

INNER WORLDS OF MEDITATION

In this self-help guide to meditation, meditation practices are transformed into valuable and practical resources for exploring the spiritual realms and dealing with life more effectively. Included are a variety of meditations that can be used for gaining spiritual awareness, achieving greater relaxation, balancing the emotions, and increasing energy.

Softbound Book #0914829459, **$11.95**
3-CD packet #0914829645, **$30**

LOVING EACH DAY FOR PEACEMAKERS: CHOOSING PEACE EVERYDAY

Peace? It's a noble idea, yet a seemingly elusive reality. Peace between nations is built upon peace between individuals, and peace between individuals depends upon peace within each person. Making peace more than just a theory or idea, Loving Each Day For Peacemakers *guides readers to their own solutions for experiencing peace.*

Hardbound book #1893020142, **$12**

PSYCHIC PROTECTION

In this book, John-Roger describes some of the invisible levels: the power of thoughts, the unconscious, elemental energies, and magic. More important, he discusses how to protect yourself against negativity that can be part of those levels. As you practice the simple techniques in this book, you can create a greater sense of well-being in and around you.

Softbound Book #0914829696, **$6.95**

172

AUDIO MATERIALS

LIVING IN GRACE

This 4 CD Packet includes the following titles:

ARE YOU LIVING UNDER LAW OR GRACE?

"People under grace are after freedom...they're saying, 'Your freedom is your choice. Be as free as you can be and I'll take the same privilege to myself.' "

CONSCIOUSNESS OF GRACE

"Getting into grace is very, very easy. Let go and let God and it's done."

FORGIVENESS INNERPHASING

"You realize that forgiveness is one of the most dynamic means you have to create inner renewal because it allows you to resolve inner conflicts and to dispense with judgments, negativity or limitations."

MEDITATION ON FORGIVENESS

"This is a meditation for healing past hurts where you may have felt disturbance with loved ones, with difficult situations, or with yourself."

FREE-FORM WRITING

"This is a form of kinesthetic writing where the neural impulses from the fingers are going back into the brain to release patterns in the unconscious."

MEDITATION FOR PEACE

"Allow yourself to recall the times that were perfect because you were living in your heart and you were at peace."

4-CD packet #3903-CD, **$35**

OBSERVATION, THE KEY TO LETTING GO

"Observation," John-Roger says, "is the key to letting go and letting God." In observation, we are not getting involved with our emotions or bringing preconceived assumptions to the situation. Learning how to practice these principles more effectively can have tangible and profound benefits for bringing greater balance and happiness into our lives.

CD #1552, **$10**

173

WHAT IS THE ULTIMATE SERVICE?

Ever get a headache and wonder where you got it? In this seminar, John-Roger talks about those experiences we have which we can trace back (sometimes) to the difficulties someone else is having. Your headache might be a form of service you're doing without even knowing it—taking on some of an experience for someone else. Could it be that God uses us to assist others in ways we don't see? "Wait until it happens to you," J-R says.

CD #7619-CD, **$10**

ARE YOU AVAILABLE TO YOURSELF?

Health, wealth, happiness, abundance, and riches are our heritage in this life. John-Roger reminds us that everything is available to us if we are available to ourselves and the spiritual life-force within us all.

CD #7238-CD, **$10**
DVD #7238-DVD, **$20**

John-Roger's books are available in bookstores everywhere. To order audio materials, contact MSIA at **1-800-899-2665**, **1-323-737-4055**, order@**msia**.org, or simply visit the online store at www.**msia**.org

174

SOUL AWARENESS DISCOURSES— A COURSE IN SOUL TRANSCENDENCE

Soul Awareness Discourses are designed to teach Soul Transcendence, which is becoming aware of yourself as a Soul and as one with God, not as a theory, but as a living reality. They are for people who want a consistent, time-proven approach to their spiritual unfoldment.

A set of Soul Awareness Discourses consists of 12 booklets, one to study and contemplate each month of the year. As you read each Discourse, you can activate an awareness of your Divine essence and deepen your relationship with God.

Spiritual in essence, Discourses are compatible with religious beliefs you might hold. In fact, most people find that Discourses support the experience of whatever path, philosophy, or religion (if any) they choose to follow. Simply put, Discourses are about eternal truths and the wisdom of the heart.

The first year of Discourses addresses topics ranging from creating success in the world to working hand-in-hand with Spirit.

A yearly set of Discourses is regularly $100. MSIA is offering the first year of Discourses at an introductory price of $50. Discourses come with a full, no-questions-asked, money-back guarantee. If at any time you decide this course of study is not right for you, simply return it, and you will promptly receive a full refund.

*To order Discourses, contact the Movement of Spiritual Inner Awareness at **1-800-899-2665**, order@**msia**.org or visit the online store at www.**msia**.org*

ABOUT THE AUTHORS

John-Roger, D.S.S.

A teacher and lecturer of international stature, John-Roger is an inspiration in the lives of many people around the world. For over four decades, his wisdom, humor, common sense and love have helped people to discover the Spirit within themselves and find health, peace, and prosperity.

With two co-authored books on the New York Times Bestseller List to his credit, and more than four dozen self-help books and audio albums, John-Roger offers extraordinary insights on a wide range of topics. He is the founder and spiritual adviser of the nondenominational Church of the Movement of Spiritual Inner Awareness (MSIA), which focuses on Soul Transcendence; founder, first president, and now chancellor of the University of Santa Monica; founder and president of Peace Theological Seminary & College of Philosophy; founder and chairman of the board of Insight Seminars; founder and spiritual adviser of the Institute for Individual and World Peace; and founder of The Heartfelt Foundation.

John-Roger has given over 6,000 lectures and seminars worldwide, many of which are televised nationally on his cable program, *That Which Is*, through the Network of Wisdoms. He has appeared on numerous radio and television shows and been a featured guest on *Larry King Live*. He also co-wrote and co-produced the movie Spiritual Warriors. (www.spiritualwarriors.com)

An educator and minister by profession, John-Roger continues to transform lives by educating people in the wisdom of the spiritual heart.

For more information about John-Roger, you may also visit: www.john-roger.org

Paul Kaye, D.S.S.

Paul Kaye has been a dedicated student of spiritual thought and practices since his youth in England. His explorations have taken him into Yoga, Zen, and the spiritual foundations of movement and the martial arts.

Paul's interests include the philosophies of such poets and teachers as Lao Tzu, Rumi and Kabir and the esoteric teachings of Jesus Christ. Paul has designed workshops on the practical application of spiritual principles and presented them worldwide. Paul is a unique and remarkable presence. He brings an abundance of lightheartedness into whatever he does, and his presentations are inspiring, practical, and filled with a wonderful sense of humor and wisdom.

For over 30 years he has studied with renowned educator and author John-Roger and he is president of the Church of the Movement of Spiritual Inner Awareness (MSIA), an ecumenical, non-denominational church. Paul is an ordained minister and has a doctorate in spiritual science.

ACKNOWLEDGMENTS

Our thanks and appreciation go to the following people whose dedication and loving brought this book about: Barbara Wieland for her enormously helpful research in the John-Roger library and archives; Vincent Dupont whose support and guidance saw this book to its completion; Stephen Keel whose skillful touches added so much; Nancy O'Leary who generously volunteered her time to edit; and Virginia Rose for patiently proofreading.

For author interviews & speaking engagements:

Please contact Angel Gibson at:

Mandeville Press

P.O. Box 513935
Los Angeles, CA 90051-1935
323-737-4055 x155

angel@mandevillepress.org

We welcome your comments and questions.

Mandeville Press
P.O. Box 513935
Los Angeles, CA 90051-1935
323-737-4055
jrbooks@**mandeville**press.org
www.**mandeville**press.org